BEHIND HER VISION

WOMEN *of* NEW YORK CITY

Ashika Kalra & Jade Chen

CONTENTS

I ALONE CANNOT CHANGE THE WORLD, BUT I CAN CAST A STONE ACROSS THE WATERS TO CREATE MANY RIPPLES.

Mother Teresa

conquer

ALEXIS
KASHAR

Alexis Kashar is a Deaf civil rights and special education attorney who founded RoseBYANDER, a company that produces Love Sign statement jewelry symbolizing equality and unity for the Deaf community. She is also cofounder of AlertBOSS, a technology startup that develops accessible emergency alerts for individuals who are deaf or hard of hearing. Prior to starting her two companies, Alexis was a civil rights attorney who championed public access for people who are deaf, hard of hearing or disabled. Alexis is the President of the Board of Trustees for the New York School for the Deaf and has formerly served as the public policy chair for the National Association of the Deaf.

MIDTOWN

I WAS BORN DEAF. CHALLENGES WERE THE NORM FOR ME.

But I've never faced a problem I didn't want to try to solve. That includes working with the NFL to enact change in Super Bowl commercials.

I met someone with close connections to the NFL at a party. We were discussing how the best part of the Super Bowl is the commercials, but the law didn't require them to be captioned. He was surprised: "You don't have access to the commercials?" I said, "No . . . and neither do forty-eight million other people." He immediately set up a meeting between me and the NFL.

I brought representatives from the National Association of the Deaf with me to the meeting, where we discussed how simple and inexpensive it was to caption the commercials. The NFL was extremely accommodating—they really wanted to be as inclusive as possible, even if the law didn't require it.

Afterward, the NFL enacted a policy that would encourage advertisers to caption their commercials. Initially, about 10 percent of commercials were captioned but within a few years, that shot up to 100 percent.

Advocacy has always been a part of me. My parents, who are both deaf, were always looking to make the world a better place. When we moved from New York City to Texas, my mother went from being a homemaker to a cofounder, with my father, of an assistive technology manufacturing business.

They manufactured portable devices that captured important household sounds and delivered alerts through visual and haptic systems. These were for everyday sounds that hearing people often take for granted: a baby crying, a phone ringing, a fire alarm. My parents showed me what it meant to live advocacy by example.

After we settled in Texas, my parents decided it was time for me to get a sign language interpreter for my classes. Until then, I never had full access in a classroom. From kindergarten until the end of middle school, I sat in the front row and depended on my lip reading skills to follow along. I also relied heavily on books to get me through.

At the local public school, administrators said that although they hadn't provided interpreters to students in the past, they'd try it out for me. And just like that, I started high school experiencing—for the first time—how easy communication could be. I was able to follow not only the teachers' instructions in real time but also conversations going on in the classroom. Understanding comments made by my peers showed me that my own thoughts and feelings were shared by others. And that gave me the confidence to participate in extracurricular activities like student government and cheerleading.

But within just one year, the school decided they wouldn't provide the interpreters anymore. It was getting too expensive. They said it was time for me to be placed in what they called a "regional program" for the deaf, which focused on vocational training.

That was *not* for me.

My parents challenged the school district, and after a very lengthy battle, we won. Thankfully, the law required my school to provide interpreters throughout the legal dispute, so I was able to continue my classes.

> This was the moment I decided I would go to law school. I realized how important it is for students to receive services that accommodate their needs. I wanted to represent others with disabilities and fight for their rights.

As a civil rights lawyer, I felt especially connected to working with deaf children and adults who experienced discrimination in public places.

I could really understand what they were going through, and I was proud to support their families beyond what was required of me as a lawyer. But the biggest area of pride for me was making real changes to civil rights law for people with disabilities.

Then after nearly two decades in practice, I took some time off to focus on my young kids. I always knew I'd go back to work someday, but when that day came, I felt my priorities shift. I still wanted to make lasting contributions in the world, but to go beyond the limitations of law. I found myself frustrated with the constraints of this field. It seemed too institutionalized and frozen in time for me to create change through the mediums that people understand today. I didn't fully recognize it then, but what I really wanted was entrepreneurship.

During a business trip to Asia with my mother and sister, we made a family heirloom necklace that represented our relationship with the deaf community and our love for American Sign Language (ASL). As I wore my piece, I can't tell you how many times I was approached by strangers who'd say, "My brother or sister is deaf," or "I learned ASL in high school." It opened up a world of stories I never knew existed and it inspired me to launch RoseBYANDER, a jewelry collection that bridges the ASL community with the rest of the world.

At the same time, I began exploring a new kind of technology that could provide alerts to the deaf and hard of hearing in emergency situations. We've already finished the app, prototype, and experiments for this product and are gearing up for investor backing to go to market.

I think I was born to be an entrepreneur. It just feels right. Seeing my parents build from their hearts helped me make the pivot. If they hadn't encouraged me to take another leap, I probably wouldn't have expanded my horizons beyond law and become the lawyer, entrepreneur, and activist that I am today.

Sometimes I wonder if I overdo it—but life is short. I want to see both of my companies connect people in new ways. It's something I couldn't do through practicing law alone. And even though I've worn different hats, my goal has always been the same: to make the world a better place by providing access and communication for everyone.

CREATIVITY COMES FROM SOLVING PROBLEMS.

If there is a problem that people deeply understand, can relate to, and want solved, then there is an opportunity for creating powerful impact.

Alexis Kashar

I'M NOT AFRAID OF STORMS, FOR I'M LEARNING TO SAIL MY SHIP.

Louisa May Alcott

adventure

SAMANTHA
BARRY

Samantha Barry is the editor-in-chief of the US
edition of *Glamour* magazine. In 2018, she became
the eighth editor-in-chief since the publication's
founding in 1939, and the first to have never worked
in print media before leading a Condé Nast magazine.
Prior to *Glamour,* Samantha was the Head of Social
Media for CNN and a journalist with the BBC. Born
in Cork, Ireland, Samantha started her media career
after obtaining a master's in journalism from Dublin
City University and working in radio journalism for
RTÉ, Ireland's national broadcaster. She has since
traveled the world producing programs and training
young journalists in Papua New Guinea, Myanmar,
Iraq, Nigeria, and more.

CHELSEA

I'M NOT SOMEONE WHO IS STIFLED BY LISTS OR PLANS.

———

The first time I went to Papua New Guinea, I left on a six-month work contract with the Australian Broadcasting Corporation. In the past, I'd felt a nervous fear every time I took on a new role, but this was on a whole different level—I remember feeling so nervous about traveling on the plane that I became physically sick. Papua New Guinea was a totally different world, so far from anyone I knew and the comfort of modern technology. I really had to take a leap of faith.

Sometimes, I think women who are driven can be driven by their fear. I flourish in that situation.

My six-month contract became eighteen months. I originally went to work on a radio journalism project, but then suddenly, mobile phones arrived on the scene. The radio project quickly evolved into a social project and then again into a digital project. The same thing happened in Myanmar. I was in and out of the country eight times, reporting for the BBC. In 2012, there was one ATM in Yangon. Very few people had landlines.

Media was a weekly newspaper that had to go through the government censorship board before it could go out to the people. But by early 2014, everybody had a mobile phone, including the monk checking his Facebook in Shwedagon Pagoda.

That's what it's about for me: getting up-close, front-row seats to the fast-forward of technology in countries like Papua New Guinea and Myanmar, and witnessing change in the media landscape.

When I reflect on the storytelling I've done at CNN or the BBC or here at *Glamour*, I'm always thinking globally first. Next, I'm thinking about how that story looks on different platforms. Today, people can hear, read, watch, and experience stories in so many formats, and it's my mission to make sure they are told in compelling ways.

I think that stems from the fact that I come from a nation of storytellers.

The saying goes that as soon as you land in Ireland, the Irish want to tell you a story and they want to know *your* story. Stories were central to my household when I was growing up, whether it was the number of newspapers that were being dropped off at our doorstep or the family sitting together to watch the evening news.

Stories have always been my passion, and I'm so lucky to be telling them.

Even though I always knew I wanted to be in media and storytelling, I wasn't so focused on only becoming a TV anchor or a war correspondent that I put blinders on and closed myself to other opportunities.

I wouldn't have left news to come to publishing if I were not open to what the evolution of my career in the world of storytelling could look like.

There are so many roles in media now. At CNN, I was the Head of Social Media—that wasn't even a job when I was in university. Technology has opened so many doors. Many of the jobs I did to grow my career didn't exist in the years prior.

> I think my willingness to take on new roles and step out of my comfort zone really opened up the possibilities for what I could achieve.

Not many people would have predicted my career to go from news broadcasting to running *Glamour* in the United States. It wasn't an obvious path.

But that's the thing—you have to take risks and do what scares you.

Especially early in your career.

If you can, that is the time to take pay cuts in exchange for experiences that will pay off in the long run. When I worked at RTÉ, which is Ireland's national radio broadcaster, I was one of the younger women in the newsroom and I always ended up with the fluffy stories when I really wanted to do hard reporting. Eventually, I chose to leave and take a job at another national radio station for less money to be able to do the stories I wanted.

> Don't be confined by your job description. It can be as wide or as narrow as you want it to be. The people I've seen grow in their careers have always been the ones who looked outside of the perimeter.

I'm glad that I made conscious decisions to continually grow in my job, and when I was no longer growing, I'm so glad I had the courage to leave and find another one.

But most importantly, I always put my hand up. That's not something that only girls in school should do. It's what young women should do in their careers. When I think about my peer network of women who have gone on to accomplish amazing things, we all had one point in common: we always asked to do more.

Nobody's going to give it to you—you must put your hand up. By offering to do more, you open more doors.

Be willing to change your plans.

The only constant is change. I'm not somebody defined by hitting certain goals by a certain age because I know that goalposts change. They change color. They change shape, and they change priorities.

Embrace the adventure. Of course, you must absolutely go for what you want. That drive is really important. But don't let it limit you—be open to a pivot. You might be surprised with where it leads you.

YOU CAN BUILD YOUR CONFIDENCE BY RAISING YOUR HAND.

The more you speak up, the more confident you become to do it again. Start by putting your toe in the water, then put your foot in the water, and soon enough, you'll be doing belly flops everywhere.

Samantha Barry

EVERY GREAT DREAM
BEGINS WITH A
DREAMER.
ALWAYS REMEMBER,
YOU HAVE WITHIN YOU
THE STRENGTH,
THE PATIENCE, AND THE
PASSION TO REACH FOR
THE STARS TO CHANGE
THE WORLD.

Harriet Tubman

dreamer

ERIN
BAGWELL

Erin Bagwell is the director and producer of *Dream, Girl*, a documentary showcasing the stories of inspiring and ambitious female entrepreneurs. *Dream, Girl* raised $100K on Kickstarter in thirty days and premiered at the White House. In 2016, Erin was named on Oprah's SuperSoul 100 list alongside honorees like Arianna Huffington, Ava DuVernay, and Lin-Manuel Miranda. Erin also founded Feminist Wednesday, a storytelling platform that features feminist stories, interviews, and insights from around the world, and she cohosts a weekly podcast called *BeaverTalk* with Diana Matthews, where they give Hollywood unsolicited advice about feminism.

KOS KAFFE, BROOKLYN

THE ELECTRICITY YOU FEEL FROM SHARING YOUR WORK IS ADDICTING.

———

I knew I would chase that feeling for the rest of my life. But the creative journey is not easy. I'll never forget when my two brilliant executive producers, Linda Goldstein Knowlton and Bous De Jong, saw my first cut of *Dream, Girl* and said, "You're going to have to cut about six people from this movie. There is so much happening that we can't emotionally connect to any one journey."

It was horrifying to hear. We were running out of time and money. There was immense pressure hanging over me, but we went back to the drawing board, reshooting scenes and recrafting the story. It was really arduous. By this point, we'd run out of funds, so I took on the job of an assistant editor, cutting scenes by the millisecond and tuning audio tracks. It became endless hours of monotonous tasks.

To fight the fatigue, I would listen to stories and podcasts about people who had finished projects and tell myself that if I could make it through this week, then I could make it through another.

I also found continued inspiration in the women entrepreneurs we featured in the film. Hearing them in my head all day as I edited every single frame pushed me to keep going. Despite watching the film thousands of times by this point, some moments would still make me laugh or cry. I think that's a testament to how open and wonderful these women were. I knew the world had to see this.

My filmmaking journey began after I was verbally harassed at work. That changed my perspective forever.

When I was harassed the first time, I thought it must've been because I was too young or too ambitious. Or because of the timbre of my voice or what I was wearing. We take it all on: "It must be *me*." Then I started realizing that my story wasn't unique. Knowing that gave me power to say, "Okay, this is the way the game is played. Now, what am I going to do about it?"

I started Feminist Wednesday as something to look forward to after my horrible nine-to-five. I was able to go home and dive into stories from incredible women entrepreneurs and showcase their work on my blog.

There wasn't any one moment that made me realize I needed to get out of my job. I just started noticing that I was dressing differently and not speaking up in meetings. I started changing my personality, which was the biggest red flag. Work is such an integral part of my identity and I didn't like the person I was becoming. I spoke to my partner, Sal, and we decided that I should figure out how to monetize Feminist Wednesday and build something for myself.

I didn't know where I needed to be, but I knew where I was not supposed to be, and that was a good enough starting point to trust myself and to trust the process.

A few months after I quit, I got this lightning-bolt idea that literally sent chills down my spine. The women sharing their stories on Feminist Wednesday were so incredible, but you couldn't see or feel them.

I have a background in video production. I thought, what if I took my passion for filmmaking and combined it with my feminist obsession to showcase female entrepreneurs in a documentary? *Dream, Girl* was born.

The idea of creating a feature-length film was daunting. It takes a lot of people and money. Everything felt so fragile and scary in the beginning. I spent the first six months just preparing for a Kickstarter campaign. A lot of people think that once you've put a Kickstarter up, money just comes in, but you actually have to network your butt off. I put $4,000 of my own savings into hiring an all-female crew and shooting a trailer for the campaign.

I'd estimated that I'd need $57,000 for the project, but within thirty days, we raised over $100,000. People responded so viscerally to the film's message. They not only wanted this—they needed it. There was so much momentum from the community, so even when we had to gut the middle of the film and start over, it made me become that much more intentional about the stories we were sharing. It was for them, and that lit a fire in me to keep hustling. Despite the ups, downs, and my creative exhaustion near the end, I never doubted that we would finish.

> We can't have it all tomorrow. All we can do is keep moving forward today, even if the steps seem really, really small.

I truly believe the universe conspires to help you gain momentum on your path, even through the small things.

Dream, Girl premiered at the White House in 2016—two and a half years after the Kickstarter campaign launched my empowerment journey. I was sweating profusely the entire time and squeezing my mother's hand. All the women in the film came, along with their families. This was my big dream—a film that has every inch of my identity in it. It was one of the best days of my life because I felt like I was finally able to give back to these women in the way that they had given to me on set.

It's a tough climb upward to create something new, but you have to trust that the energy is moving forward, even if it feels like you're being tested every step along the way.

IF YOU'VE
WAITED UNTIL
YOU'RE PREPARED,
THEN YOU'VE
WAITED
TOO LONG.

Erin Bagwell

———————

NEVER DOUBT THAT A SMALL GROUP OF THOUGHTFUL, COMMITTED CITIZENS CAN CHANGE THE WORLD. INDEED, IT'S THE ONLY THING THAT EVER HAS.

Margaret Mead

humanity

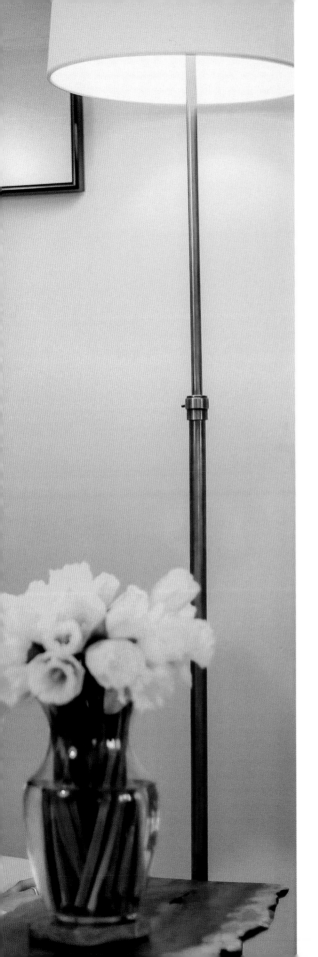

LIZ
DEE

Liz Dee is co-president and co-owner of the iconic Smarties Candy Company. She is also cofounder and CEO of Baleine & Bjorn Capital, an investment company that focuses on creating superior plant-based and cultured products. Liz also founded Vegan Ladyboss, a global collective that worked to empower and support vegan women in advancing their careers as well as animal advocacy.

WEST VILLAGE

I WAS TOLD TO HIDE THE FACT THAT SMARTIES IS FEMALE–OWNED.

———

It was the worst advice I've ever received and speaks to a misogynistic culture plaguing us today, especially evident with social media providing the shield of anonymity.

There will always be people, some who don't even know you, that disagree with the things you say and do. And that's part of life. It's part of being a leader. But the more singularly focused you are on your own goals and vision, while remaining flexible, the less the contrarians and critics will hold you back.

If anything, you rise stronger because you can address them head-on: "Yes, it may be surprising for some to see a female-run business of Smarties' size. It's unfortunate anyone may see this as unusual because this is the future. Women are roughly half of the population, and we should be seen proportionately in leadership positions."

I didn't always know that I wanted to work at the Smarties Candy Company, but once I began dipping my toe into the family business, I realized that it was a good fit for me. It's a place where I could contribute and, of course, work with my family.

Smarties was founded by my grandfather, Edward Dee, in 1949. Every day at Smarties is different, but there's always a lot of candy involved. I oversee the company with my sister and my cousin.

Together, we three women are proud to be at the helm of a third-generation family business.

This is a pretty unconventional structure. But the benefit of having three people is that you never end up with a tie, so the majority rules.

So far, this arrangement has worked for us. In addition to executive oversight, I oversee food quality and safety, and communications. When people ask me what it's like to work with family, I have to warn them that just because it works for us doesn't mean it will work for everyone. It could get complicated, and I would never recommend that anyone work with family unless they get along well and trust each other.

The most important thing that working with family has taught me is to value contribution. What can I contribute to this world? Answering that question is my guiding principle.

A few years ago, our customers began asking whether Smarties' products were vegan or vegetarian. At the time, I was only vaguely aware of the difference. I began to do my own research, which led me to videos of how we raise and slaughter animals for food and other products. I couldn't unsee that.

My husband embraced veganism with me, and in January 2016, we launched Baleine & Bjorn Capital to invest in companies that provide plant-based alternatives to outdated animal products. Through Baleine & Bjorn Capital, we're essentially angel investors, taking on the risk to buy mission-driven companies more time to attract larger capital. We've invested in more than a dozen companies, and it's been an exhilarating ride that also led me down the path of unwittingly founding another platform, Vegan Ladyboss.

Vegan Ladyboss started as a passion project. I had no idea it was going to grow the way it did. It started with five women in my apartment, having dinner and talking about how we could empower one another in our vegan lifestyle and our careers. Then it grew into a global community, with thousands of vegan women coming together for animal advocacy. Many are vegan lady bosses who quit corporate and traditional jobs to launch businesses in support of animal welfare.

This is how I see myself making a difference to the big picture. Even though I'm a company executive, I don't want to soullessly punch in and punch out every day.

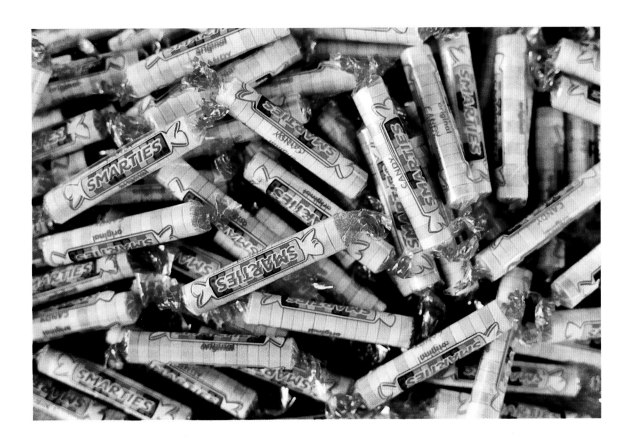

I see the contributions I make to Smarties, to veganism, to small businesses, as the most important and meaningful things I could do. This is the life of my design.

I think it's important for everyone to live a life of their own design. But not everyone will do what it takes to make it happen.

It takes planning. It takes goal setting. It takes looking at your calendar and setting the benchmarks: "Taking step A will lead to goal B tomorrow, C next week, and D next year."

Putting in the work will always make the difference. Discipline is what allows us to transcend who we used to be in order to become who we want to be.

I may not be good enough to achieve the end result today, but I'm at least good enough to achieve the milestones in between. Rather than seeing your goals as unattainable simply because you can't attain them right away, add "yet" to the end of the sentence. Suddenly, "I'm not good enough" becomes progress you could measure.

It was attaining the goals I had earlier in my career that gave me the confidence to reach higher. Continuing to work toward new challenges was what put me on a path to successes I never thought possible. It bears mentioning that I was lucky to have had certain career opportunities, but I also worked to earn my responsibilities. I'm a woman who leads an incredible company, invests in meaningful businesses, and gives back where I can.

I'm a woman who is building the life of her dreams.

NEARLY ANYTHING IS POSSIBLE IF YOU'RE HARDWORKING.

Often, we are surprised
when our wish comes true but
it is because we underestimate
ourselves and the power of
our intent.

Liz Dee

REAL CHANGE, ENDURING CHANGE, HAPPENS ONE STEP AT A TIME.

Ruth Bader Ginsburg

elevate

CLAUDIA *ROMO EDELMAN*

Claudia Romo Edelman is a Mexican-Swiss diplomat, advocate, and social entrepreneur. For over twenty-five years, she has advanced humanitarian causes in global organizations such as UNICEF, the United Nations, the World Economic Forum, and the Global Fund. In 2017, Claudia founded We Are All Human, a New York City based nonprofit that promotes equity for Hispanics. The organization has launched initiatives such as the Hispanic Promise, a national pledge in collaboration with the World Economic Forum for business leaders and US companies to create more inclusive work environments. Claudia is also a founder and cohost of *Global GoalsCast*, a podcast that highlights progress in the international community through stories of champions who are making a difference.

UPPER WEST SIDE

ALL MY LIFE, PEOPLE TOLD ME, "YOU'RE SO LOUD. DON'T BE SO LOUD."

When I was fourteen, Mexico City faced a series of earthquakes that literally destroyed 80 percent of the city. My job was to sweep the streets of my neighborhood and find people trapped under the rubble. There was so much chaos noise from sirens, ambulances, and people shouting. I thought I heard a faint little voice but I couldn't be sure. I started screaming just screaming at the top of my lungs. People in my volunteer group turned to me in a panic: "What? What is it?" I pointed and said, "There is a voice I think there is a voice here."

My group gathered around and started moving the huge stones, piece by piece, to find this voice. They couldn't hear it, but it was becoming clearer to me that it was there, so I started screaming even louder to try to get more help. When we removed the last stone, there they were: the eyes of a little girl, filled with anxiety and fear her eyelashes covered in dust. Our eyes locked. It was almost as if she said, "You got me. You got my back."

Then she climbed out and ran to her mother. All of us started crying.

It was a feeling I'd never had before. But suddenly it all made sense. I was meant to be loud. I was meant to use my voice and bring attention to the things that mattered. I felt useful for the first time in my life, and I would spend the next twenty-five years building a career that would bring a voice to the voiceless.

When you're young, it can be hard to be completely sure about what you want to do, and that's okay.

But have clarity on who you *are*.

I'm loud, so I make a good advocate. I set agendas. I bring attention to issues in a way that's authentic to me. It was clear from early on that I cared about the world. I loved visiting countries and learning new languages. In fact, I couldn't wait to leave. So much so that I practically left the country with my prom dress on.

My mom's friend worked at an embassy in Switzerland, and through her, I started a job as a diplomat, representing Mexico abroad.

I'm grateful that my very first job was in line with my early passions. Living in other countries allowed me to experience being an insider and outsider at the same time. I learned six languages on the go. Assimilating into so many different countries and cultures developed my muscle for adaptability and honed my survival instincts in a way that made life very enriching.

A few years ago, I worked in the Executive Office of the Secretary-General of the United Nations. I started looking at my Hispanic community and realized that we had very few role models and heroes. Even though I'd been speaking a lot and championing important humanitarian efforts, my impact had all been from behind the scenes and for agendas set by others. I hadn't been a leader.

My father used to fly our family over Mexico and I would be his copilot, reading the maps for him by his side. He would always say, "You're a great copilot." I loved hearing him say that and I believed it.

But over the years, I became too comfortable as a copilot. I started wondering: What if I became a pilot? A pilot of my own life, setting my own agendas.

I could inspire my community to do more. We work like hell but we don't speak up. We don't bark. We don't bite. We don't even vote. All because it feels uncomfortable.

Hispanics are the muscle of America's middle class. We bring jobs, hard work, passion, and opportunities. Hispanics represent 12 percent of US GDP, and together we are the seventh-largest economy in the world—larger than India. We don't need to fake it. We have it. In this lifetime, I want to see a Hispanic community empowered and united. No more Mexicans versus Colombians versus Venezuelans—just one Hispanic community supporting each other.

In 2017, I made a major decision to step out from big organizations and create my own foundation, We Are All Human, to speak up for the Hispanic community and become a leader rather than just speak about leadership. We created the Hispanic Promise, a first-of-its-kind national pledge to hire, promote, and retain Hispanics in the workplace. It's a call to action for corporate America to create a more inclusive work environment.

As a humanitarian, I know change is possible because I've seen it. I rescued a girl from the earthquake. I've championed for causes in my career and seen their impact by the numbers. If I know change is within reach, why would I stop now?

I'd never imagined how much fun, impact, and purpose I could have as my own pilot. Now my voice is at the forefront. I tell my daughter, when you look at the sky, know that it's further than you think. So aim high—and then higher. It's your vision that drives action. Your ideas ignite you toward where you want to go. But first, ask, "Who am I?" And make that a part of what you do.

Let your strengths be your guiding force. Sure, mitigate your weaknesses, but don't focus on them too much. They don't define you, and they certainly won't define your limits.

THE WOMEN I ADMIRE NEVER HAD ANYTHING JUST FALL INTO THEIR LAPS.

They are *always* striving for what's next and consider every challenge a learning opportunity.

Claudia Romo Edelman

—————

I BELIEVE THAT POTENTIAL IS UNLIMITED – SUCCESS DEPENDS ON DARING TO ACT ON DREAMS.

Estée lauder

original

CHELSEY *WHITE*

Chelsey White is a self-taught baker, blogger, and social media influencer. She is the founder of Chelsweets, an online and social media platform known for time-lapse video tutorials on baking, icing, and decorating eye-catching cakes, cupcakes, and cookies. Her sixty-second videos have received millions of views across TikTok, YouTube, and Instagram. Chelsey has been featured in the *Wall Street Journal, Bloomberg, Business Insider, Cosmopolitan, Yahoo!,* and more.

MIDTOWN EAST

I LIKED HAVING TWO CAREERS AT ONCE. IT FELT SAFE.

———

Quitting public accounting wasn't something I worked toward. It was kind of in the back of my mind. I'd set goals for Chelsweets, but they were the kind I didn't think I would ever hit. I might've done that on purpose so that I could use not hitting them as an excuse to stay in accounting. I liked my job. I liked the financial security it provided me.

But then Chelsweets started hitting those benchmarks—an income target, a number of partnerships, and different revenue streams. And I couldn't keep doing both jobs.

I mean—I *could*. I just wasn't sleeping.

A bunch of Instagram partnerships came to me at once, I was making a ton of content for the Food Network, and my day job became even more demanding. It was all so overwhelming. After a certain point, I knew I could no longer give my best to either role.

I realized that I don't need to prove to the world I can do everything at once. And that's okay.

The funny thing is, I don't really know where my passion for baking comes from. I didn't grow up baking. The closest memory I have is making cupcakes from a boxed mix for friends' birthday parties. My mom didn't spend a lot of time in the kitchen. Both of my parents worked a lot. A fun fact is that I still don't know how to cook—at all. I don't like touching meat. It scares me.

Baking really started for me after college. I moved from Seattle to New York City to work in accounting. After staring at Excel for sixteen hours a day, I felt like I *needed* to do something else. I'd always loved art projects, and now that I finally had my own kitchen, I could play around in there, use my hands, and exercise a different side of my brain.

I remember feeling very proud of my first cake: "I made that from scratch. This is great. Tastes good." I posted it on Instagram in the same way people want to share a really good meal. I wanted to remember the experience and show others: "Look what I spent all day making. I'm proud of it."

It was never my intention to sell cakes. I happened to bake one for a friend's birthday at work one day. People on my team ended up loving it and asked if I would bake them another. Then other teams started asking me to bake them cakes. Guests at friends' parties would come up to me trying to order a cake for their next event. I charged next to nothing. I barely covered my ingredients' cost.

I was reluctant at first but the more I baked, the more I fell in love with it. I began obsessing over new techniques and decorating.

My first cake that went viral was one I baked for a friend's birthday. I called it "one glass too many." It was a red wine cake with a wine glass shoved into the side and red ganache dripping down, like the wine had spilled.

I thought it was really funny but the internet went wild. The video received four million views when I had only fifty thousand followers. It was a huge reach. Being an accountant and all about numbers, I was freaking out watching the followers, views, and likes grow. It was magical.

But as more time passed, excitement gave way to a slow grind. I would frequently bake until 1:00 a.m. and then get up early the next day to go into work. And when I had to stay late in the office, I would feel a crushing pressure to know I still had to bake later that night. Things like that can really dampen the intensity of your passion over time.

Eventually, I hit a wall. I couldn't keep up with the growth of Chelsweets while maintaining my day job and my sanity.

There was a lot of back-and-forth going on in my head. I would practice a great resignation speech to my boss and then go right back to convincing myself that I could do it all.

I was also anxious about the career transition. How would I introduce myself at parties? As an influencer? There were so many negative associations with that, especially when I was starting out.

> I talked about it a lot with my family, friends, and husband. While the decision is never easy, the person I had the hardest time convincing that everything would be okay was *me*.

One of the biggest uncertainties for young entrepreneurs is when to quit the day job. How far along does my business need to be?

It really comes down to your idea.

I was able to develop Chelsweets to a stable point while maintaining my day job, but if you're building a business that requires your full dedication, then you might need to commit to one path much earlier. No matter where you are in the journey, just be aware of when you're trying to do too much out of fear.

Before I quit my job, I never thought I'd be doing private cake lessons or teaching at the Institute of Culinary Education. But once I committed to mastering my craft, I found boundless creativity in trying new things, growing different revenue streams, and creating content that people love.

Once you commit to doing one thing well, you will begin seeing inspiration everywhere.

A LOT OF US IN NEW YORK CITY WANT TO DO IT ALL:

I can do this, I can do that—
all at *the same time.* It makes you feel
powerful and capable. But just because
you can doesn't mean you should.

Chelsey White

DREAM AND GIVE YOURSELF PERMISSION TO ENVISION A YOU THAT YOU CHOOSE TO BE.

Joy Page

character

BATOULY
CAMARA

Batouly Camara is a professional basketball player, coach, author, and founder of Women and Kids Empowerment (WAKE), a nonprofit that works to educate and empower young girls in Guinea, West Africa, and New York City. Batouly played Division I basketball for the University of Connecticut and is the head basketball coach at Blair Academy in New Jersey. In 2020, she was honored with the Billie Jean King Youth Leadership Award, and in 2021, she was named a *Forbes* 30 Under 30 in Sports. Batouly also authored *A Basketball Game on Wake Street,* which promotes diversity and inclusion through sport.

HUDSON YARDS

I FELL IN LOVE WITH BASKETBALL THROUGH SISTERHOOD.

———————

When I was twelve, I walked past a park and saw a girl who seemed like an absolute giant. She was six foot three. I asked, "Where did you get your jeans from?" She happily responded and then said, "You're so tall, you should play basketball." I was about five foot eight at the time.

I started coming by the park every day after school. We'd shoot hoops and then order pizza. She took me in and I've played basketball ever since.

Basketball didn't come easy to me and it still doesn't. But I think that's where the love grew. They say to pursue what sets your soul on fire. That was basketball for me. It was the one thing I couldn't stop thinking about. Sure, there were moments when it got tough and I wanted to quit. But they never lasted more than a day. Basketball was my haven.

I went to my first WNBA game when I was fourteen. It was at Madison Square Garden. Watching the game live made it that much more real. Girls can play basketball. The feeling was so overwhelming that I thought I could cry. The crowd and the experience—I wanted it all so badly.

After I got home, I went on the McDonald's All American and ESPN Top 100 websites and scrolled through the girls. I knew I could be one of them. Then I set up a webcam and just started crying, "I just want to be there. I just want to be *there*." There was no one on the other side. It was just me pleading with the universe.

I look back on that memory and laugh because it's like, "Wow, you did it. You actually did it."

We don't always think of those moments in our journey: why we ever started. But the why can't be silenced even in your deepest struggle. It's what keeps you going.

My biggest hurdle initially was getting my family to value my passion. We are first-generation immigrants from Guinea, West Africa. My father had two PhDs and my mom always said, "Basketball can be taken away any second, but no one can take your diploma. No one can take away what you've learned and who you are."

They didn't have an issue with the sport itself. It's just that they didn't see how it could be a viable career path. Then I said, "I can get a full scholarship to college through basketball." Before long, basketball became "an amazing opportunity."

I started playing college basketball at the University of Kentucky and then transferred after my freshman year to the University of Connecticut, where I was a forward for the Division I team.

I faced a lot of injuries. It started with shoulder surgery. Then, in my junior year, I started having issues with my knees to a point where they lost stability and I needed to learn to walk again. Losing something I took so much for granted and then getting it back made me realize that all of this can be taken away in a second. I was so grateful just to have another day.

> You hear about people who have career-ending injuries. . . . It started to make me think about what my life would look like after basketball.

In school I was once asked, "Who are you without naming your sport?" I had an internal breakdown because thirty minutes went by and I still couldn't come up with an answer. Then the facilitator said, "You're a great sister. You're a great friend. You're bilingual. How do you lean into those?" I spent forty hours a week on basketball. How could I work on developing *me?*

In 2017, I took a three-month trip to Guinea to rediscover my roots and learn about basketball there. The experience was mirrors and windows—a mirror of myself and a window into other girls. The struggle in getting my own family to value sport was society at large for these girls.

Most said they couldn't see the endgame. Their families undermined their efforts because basketball wasn't seen as a viable career.

One girl said, "I don't want to be handed anything. Just give me the opportunity to fight for my dreams." It was heartbreaking. That's what I *said* as a fourteen-year-old in front of that webcam. But there were almost no resources or opportunities for these girls to fight with. I couldn't awaken a dream within a little girl and leave it as is. That was just not fair.

On my flight back to New York, a quote came to mind: "I don't want to reinvent the wheel. I just want to keep it spinning." Sport changed my life. How can we keep it spinning in Guinea? That's when I decided to create Women and Kids Empowerment (WAKE). Every girl should be able to play sports. It took tremendous resources, support, and mentorship for me to become the player I am. You can't be who you can't see.

How do we create more access, opportunities, and resources for young girls in and outside of basketball?

WAKE began by running camps to empower girls through holistic development. One exercise I do is ask them to imagine that someone gave them a million dollars. What would you do? No dream is too big. If we don't train ourselves to think that way, then it becomes too easy to stop expanding and live in fear.

Some people don't mature. They just get older. I want to mature.

WAKE has helped me grow and develop an identity beyond my wildest dreams. When I was down from my injuries in college, all I could think about was what my life would look like on the other side. *Who am I?*

Now it's clear: I am Batouly Camara, and I fight for spaces where women and kids can dream beyond their realities.

DON'T JUST TRUST THE PROCESS. STAY PRESENT IN IT.

If you trust blindly, you'll go in with your head down. If you stay present, you start to know yourself and that's how you grow through the experience.

Batouly Camara

———

DO ONE THING EVERY DAY THAT SCARES YOU.

Eleanor Roosevelt

bravery

JESSICA *DULONG*

Jessica DuLong is an author, a Coast Guard–licensed Merchant Marine officer, and chief engineer of the iconic New York City fireboat *John J. Harvey.* She was the only female fireboat engineer to serve during 9/11 and has been recognized for her service in the *Congressional Record*. Jessica's writing has been honored by the American Society of Journalists and Authors; her most recent book is *Saved at the Seawall: Stories from the September 11 Boat Lift.*

BROOKLYN BRIDGE PARK PIER 6

September 11, 2001

IT WAS A DAY OF RECKONING AND LOSS OF INNOCENCE.

I didn't get the chance to assist until the next day, but when I did, I actually felt a sense of relief. Finally, there was a way for me to serve and contribute.

I caught a ride from merchant marines on a pontoon boat. They tossed me a spare life jacket, and it was huge. I stood at the edge of the boat and held on tight as we crashed through the waves.

My jacket flapping away in the wind symbolized how I felt in that moment: not big enough. I wasn't big enough for the challenge that lay ahead.

As the boat plowed through the water, smoke from Ground Zero overwhelmed my senses, even though I was still miles away. I was literally breathing in the dust of thousands and thousands of lives. That memory never fades. Maybe it's just hindsight, but I do vividly remember having this sinking feeling that nothing was ever going to be the same.

Anything I said or did next was going to be a complete break from who I had been before.

I was still new to the field, and in contrast to experienced mariners who knew on first impulse how to help the community, I was at a loss for what to do. I had spent the first twenty-four hours after the attack useless. I don't think I fully grasped the scale of the crisis until I saw it for myself. The scene was beyond comprehension.

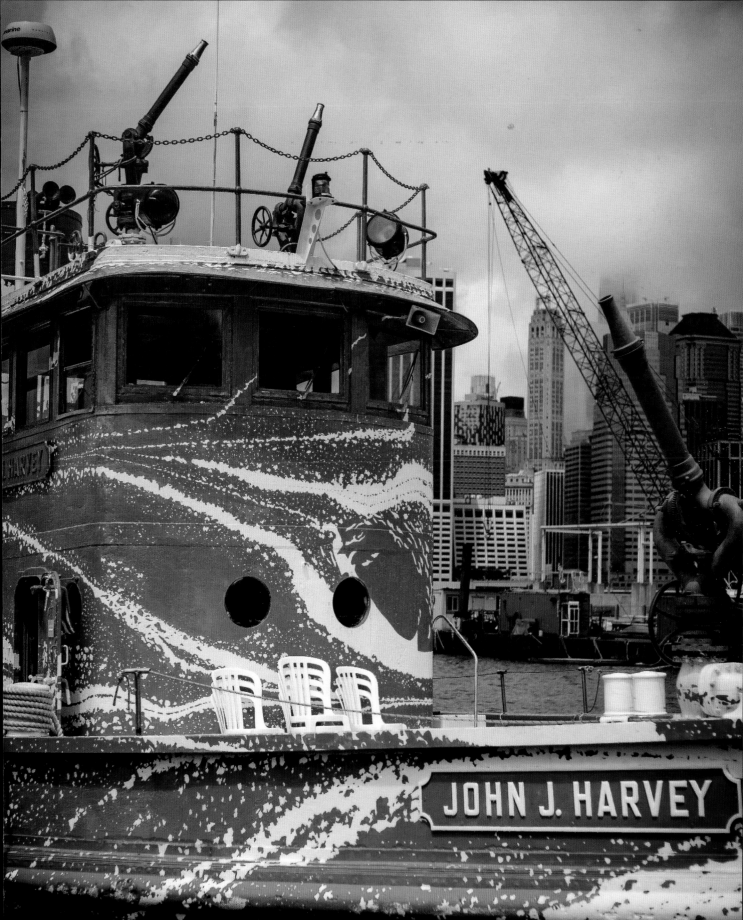

JOHN J. HARVEY

Even though I was afraid, it had always been my default to go after what I feared most.

It's like a control strategy—a way to control anxiety. What are you most afraid of? Do it. It's the surest way to overcome that fear.

I think this mindset comes from having to pivot again and again. I've had many callings in life. I think we all do. My career started out as the complete opposite of a marine engineer.

I was working for a tech startup in the dot-com era when I moved to New York City from San Francisco. It just so happened that the company I worked for was subleasing office space from an owner of the *John J. Harvey*, and we got to know each other. I was working a million hours a week and spending my life at my desk when he said one day, "Join us on the fireboat—we're going out to Bear Mountain for a fall leaf trip."

I didn't even know what those words meant. I had no concept of what a fireboat was. I didn't know where Bear Mountain was. But the first time I joined the guys on the boat, I ended up cutting out an unused pipe with a power saw on top of a massive diesel engine. I was completely taken by this experience. It felt magical. I've always had an appreciation for engines and machines, but this was unlike anything I was doing at the time.

From that day forward, the crew on the *John J. Harvey* couldn't get rid of me. I wanted to learn everything. They offered me a chance to try out as an assistant engineer, running the stand on the boat. I was all over it. The engine room would become my new domain.

But I was always reminded, intentionally or unintentionally, that being a woman in this role meant that I was viewed in a different light.

I struggled with the attention, and my mind would often divert from what I needed to do to who was going to question me and whether I belonged.

I called my mom saying, "There is not a path for someone like me to do this." She replied, "You make your own path."

Even en route to Ground Zero on the day after 9/11, I remember that there was just one seat available on the boat. The guys urged me to take it, out of courtesy. I didn't want to. It felt weird—like another reminder that I was different.

Rather than allow myself to get swept up, I just tried to refocus on what actually mattered. I wasn't there for an audience. I was there for a purpose—to help put out the fires. We didn't know it then, but fireboats were the only sources of firefighting water available because the fire hydrants were covered by rubble and the fire mains had collapsed from the impact.

There was nothing more significant than the job before me. Getting it done meant devoting my entire mental energy to it. But being in the present takes practice, and over time, it gets easier.

So much of life is about staying cool-headed as you walk through an open door. It's okay to feel uncomfortable. It's okay to ask yourself: "Am I good enough?" If you're not failing, then you're not trying hard. It means you're staying in the safe place of mastery. It's not real success if you're not learning and growing.

Don't just be open to opportunities—jump into them. Try things you're not immediately good at. Practice. And feel free to mess up, because that's part of the process too.

MY APPROACH TO FEAR IS TO JUST TAKE IT ON.

The majority of what we worry about never happens. Think about all we could achieve if we applied the energy we waste on worrying to doing.

Jessica DuLong

TO THE WRONGS
THAT NEED
RESISTANCE,
TO THE RIGHT THAT
NEEDS ASSISTANCE,
TO THE FUTURE IN
THE DISTANCE,
GIVE YOURSELVES.

Carrie Chapman Catt

honor

KHALIDA
BROHI

Khalida Brohi is an award-winning author, social entrepreneur, and activist from the Balochistan province of Pakistan. She is the founder and executive director of the Sughar Foundation, a nonprofit fighting to end exchange marriages, child marriages, and honor killings. Khalida is the author of the memoir *I Should Have Honor*, which details the personal events that inspired her career as an activist for Pakistani women's rights. *Newsweek* named Khalida on its 25 Under 25 Young Women to Watch list and *Forbes* recognized her as a 30 Under 30 honoree for social entrepreneurship. Khalida is a co-owner of The Chai Spot with her husband, David. The Chai Spot serves a variety of Pakistani chai and represents a peace-building initiative inspired by the love story between Khalida and David, an Italian American from Los Angeles.

LITTLE ITALY

ONCE I LEARNED THAT HONOR COULD KILL, I DIDN'T WANT IT ANYMORE.

———————

Growing up in the mountains of Pakistan, I fell in love with our music, dance, and vibrancy. I was especially proud of our honor—the honor that welcomes guests into our home, that donates to charity even if you are poor, and that cares for others, even strangers. But as I grew older, I started to notice another side to honor that went unexplained—one that seemed to only suppress women and girls. For example, women weren't allowed to go outside of their homes. I understood it was for our protection. But what about girls being married off at nine years old?

As the first girl in my family to go to school, I was already beginning to question our tribal norms when the unthinkable happened.

One day, I went back to my village and couldn't find my cousin, Khadija. I kept asking around: "Is she sick? Did she get married off?" No one would utter a word.

At night, when we crawled into our cots to sleep, a cousin peeked her head from under the covers and whispered, "Khadija is dead. Uncle killed her." I froze. That moment could've stretched the length of my entire life.

Not long before her murder, Khadija had confided in her mother that she was in love with someone. But it was already arranged for her to marry a cousin. No one would ever agree to a love marriage. We were taught that falling in love is a sin. So one night, Khadija snuck away to marry her love in secret. My eldest uncle sent people searching for them in every bus station and possible hiding spot.

They were instantly caught.

Khadija was brought home and locked in a room, guarded by men with guns, until her punishment was decided. My eldest uncle told his brother, Khadija's father, "You cannot show your face in this village if she's not killed for this dishonor." Their concerns were real. If Khadija's father left his home and business in shame, he wouldn't be able to feed his family. So why not sacrifice one daughter to save the whole family? Of course, none of this was discussed with the women.

Finally, Khadija's father agreed after two weeks of debate, and Khadija was taken by three men and strangled. No one got to pray for her. No one even knows where her grave is. She was just a teenager.

> I had nightmares about Khadija for a year. I was only in the ninth grade, but I decided to make sure that no other girl would be murdered in the name of honor.

I started by composing poems in both English and Urdu and reading them at local nonprofit events. I wrote from Khadija's shoes, trying to convey how she might've felt as she took her last breath—those poems were so dark and intense.

After joining some national campaigns against honor killings, I started a youth and gender development program in my village. We went door to door training young girls and boys to use a computer, speak English, and vocalize their rights. Tribal leaders quickly kicked me out. Then I returned with the Wake Up campaign against honor killings. By this point, people in the villages were just done with me—"She's challenging her own tribal culture. How dare she?" They started writing letters threatening my father, "If you don't stop her, we will."

My work took a tremendous toll on my parents over the years. It was a constant negotiation for me to do this. They reminded me that I could just as easily dishonor them and that I'd never be married off under this kind of scrutiny. Still, they didn't try to stop me until, in 2009, threats from the tribal village sent my father over the edge. He took away my internet access. I was only allowed to go to school and come home.

That was the first time I felt like I'd completely failed. I looked back on the impact of my work over the last five years and found none.

The same girls were being beaten, denied education, and married off. Other national programs fighting honor killings were similarly ineffective. Taking this step back was a blessing in disguise. I had time to research tribal law and learned that a lot of these actions are driven by peer pressure.

> Honor killings don't just kill one girl. The grief kills a whole family.

In the years following Khadija's death, her father died of a heart attack and her mother died of cancer. Then my uncle, whom I still hadn't forgiven, grew terminally ill. The turning point was when he moved in with Khadija's small siblings after her parents passed away and started caring for them as a father figure. Seeing my uncle grasp on to love in his final years opened my heart to his side of the story. I better understood just how complex our society and the tribal restrictions are. Ironically, my uncle's perspective helped me uncover the three reasons why our programs weren't working.

First, our country's policies didn't protect women. Second, men believe that women, land, and money are the property of men. The third and most powerful reason is that women let this happen. We tell each other to stay quiet and accept violence as our fate.

This whole time I had been targeting young boys, girls, and men in the tribal areas, but not the women, who needed help most.

This time, I knew what to do.

My work was to empower women with awareness of their rights and teach them the skills for self-sufficiency. This is how the Sughar Foundation was born.

For so many years, I looked outside myself for evidence of change. But change couldn't have been more evident than on my own wedding day, when I married David, an American from Los Angeles. We met in 2013 through a mutual friend during one of my visits to the city for work.

I remember those feelings I felt for him, the same ones that Khadija died for, and they terrified me. My parents vehemently rejected the idea of marriage outside our culture. Even though David had fallen in love with Islam and converted, my parents were still not convinced.

Then, in September 2014, I found a way for them to meet.

David and I invited our families to Italy, where I was speaking. Before they arrived, we canceled their hotel rooms and put them all in the same Airbnb.

It had the smallest living room. Everyone was practically in each other's laps. But through sitting together and sipping chai, our families each saw beyond the other's skin color, language, and religion. They talked, laughed, and embraced one another as human beings.

In 2015, five hundred people who once denied the concept of love marriage celebrated mine and David's over ten days. I kept thinking about Khadija, who died for the same request a decade before.

I was twenty-six. I am now pregnant with our first child at thirty-one. How far we've come. One person really can redefine the bigger picture. But we must be open to all sides of the story—even the ones that hurt.

DON'T GET STUCK ON ONE SIDE OF THE STORY.

Be curious about the bigger picture.
It wasn't until I opened myself to my
enemy's perspective that I actually
found the solution I'd been looking
for all along.

A GIRL SHOULD BE TWO THINGS: WHO AND WHAT SHE WANTS.

Coco Chanel

unfettered

NINA
DAVULURI

Nina Davuluri gained global recognition as the first-ever South Asian woman to be crowned Miss America. Since her historic win in 2014, she has been a fierce advocate for cultural competency, philanthropy, and women's rights through meaningful partnerships with the world's leading NGOs, the US Department of State, the White House and institutions such as NASA and Google. Her pioneering work has been widely acclaimed by global activists and leaders including former President Barack Obama and First Lady Michelle Obama. As a global leader in redefining beauty standards, Nina challenges beauty standards and colorism in her first documentary production, #COMPLEXion. Through her advocacy efforts, she was invited to serve on the Diversity & Inclusion Advisory Board for L'oreal USA.

OCULUS

"SO, MISS AMERICA . . . CAN YOU COOK?"

———————

This was the first question an uncle asked when I greeted him shortly after I won the title. I responded with a bit of sarcasm of my own: "Not as well as I can speak."

While most of the women in my family were going down the "good Indian" path by either getting married or becoming doctors, I had just hosted a large event at Madison Square Garden in New York. I was making strides in what was considered an "unconventional" career, speaking on platforms that mattered to me and engaging with diversity activists around the country. But one way or another, I'd find myself back in conversations that required me to justify my life and career choices, or to field questions that were actually backhanded compliments.

I have been struggling against expectations my entire life: how I should look, what I should say, and who I should be.

From an early age, I struggled to meet the beauty standards of both the US and India. I was "too dark" for Indians and "too different" for Americans. Growing up, I was constantly told to avoid the sun or that I would be "so much prettier" if my skin were just a couple of shades lighter. My college boyfriend even confessed that he worried about me meeting his mom—that she would think I was too dark.

The sad part is that while I wasn't immune to this type of commentary, I did eventually grow used to it. But when I became Miss America, discussions about the color of my skin and my "ethnic" features were no longer just among friends and family—they were global headlines. It was the peak of the Twittersphere, so everything was elevated by social media. While I had dealt with similar negativity as Miss New York, the level of hate I encountered after winning Miss America was on a whole other level. Not only was I "too dark" for Indians, I was now also not "American-looking" enough to be a Miss America.

My parents were also thrust into a new world. I grew up in a family of physicians and my mom saw the pageant win as leverage for me to attend the best medical school I could. I remember running to my mom and sister after getting off the stage. My sister was like, "You did it!" while my mom said, "Now you can get into any medical school you want!"

I absolutely adore my mother, but I just responded with a sarcastic "Yeah!"

She had her own expectations of me, focused on what I was supposed to achieve academically. But that was partly my fault. I'd told everyone that I was going to compete for Miss America and pursue medical school after. While that might've been my intention in the beginning, my dreams were starting to change. I knew in my heart that I was meant for something else, but I was afraid to articulate what that might be because it could be against my family's wishes.

Between pressure from my family and attention from the media, I was drowning in the expectations of others.

In my most vulnerable moment—right as I was about to put myself out there on stage—everyone around me started saying, 'You know, you're too Indian—be a little more American. Maybe don't do a Bollywood dance. You should go back to singing.' I can sing, but it's not who I am. I love dancing and performing. If I win, it has to be authentic to who I am.

Winning Miss America made me realize that my life really could be something different from what I had imagined and what others imagined for me.

The pageant helped me see that I didn't need to be a doctor to be successful. In fact, I didn't even want to be one. I'd only chosen that career because it was the one expected of me. I could choose otherwise and still be successful—just as I am of Indian origin and can still be Miss America.

The onus is on each one of us to live life on our terms. You have to set standards for yourself or else other people will.

I wish more people saw me at my lowest of lows as opposed to the highest of highs, because it's those low points that have defined who I am and set the stage for what I've been able to achieve. I saw an opportunity to go beyond skin deep and use my title and platform to lead as an activist, starting with conversations about diversity that I wish I'd had growing up.

People view the job of Miss America as modeling or being a pretty face. While that is certainly a component, it is largely about speaking and advocating. You have to get your message across with kindergartners, parents, CEOs, and senators alike.

In 2014, I launched Circles of Unity, a social media campaign that facilitates discussions on racial diversity at university campuses and organizations around the world. Our goal isn't just about explaining what it means to be Indian, South Asian, or any specific ethnicity. Our goal is to educate people that we are all human beings first and foremost, and that humanity is what unites us. I consider each day a "win" if I can improve one person's understanding of my mission or what a modern-day woman can achieve.

For a while, my parents didn't even believe that I had a real job. But I feel I've made a career out of defying standards. It's not an easy journey to go against the norm, but have faith that the answers are already within you. Follow your gut and stay true to your mission. You will find far more satisfaction in that than any path the world dreams up for you.

OVER THE YEARS, I HAVE FOUND CONFIDENCE WITHIN ME TO DEFY STANDARDS.

We all have the power to set a new precedent.

Nina Davuluri

YOUR SUCCESS AND HAPPINESS LIES IN YOU. RESOLVE TO KEEP HAPPY, AND YOUR JOY AND YOU SHALL FORM AN INVINCIBLE HOST AGAINST DIFFICULTIES.

Helen Keller

enoughness

LISA
CARMEN
WANG

Lisa Carmen Wang is an entrepreneur and a former
gymnast on the USA Women's National Gymnastic
Team. Lisa was a four-time US national champion
and represented the US in three Gymnastics World
Championships. In 2014, she was inducted into
the USA Gymnastics Hall of Fame. Previously, Lisa
co-founded SheWorx, a global investment platform
and event series aimed at closing the funding gap for
female founders. SheWorx held over three hundred
events and helped women raise more than $50
million in funding before being acquired by Republic,
a community investment platform. Lisa has been
featured on *Forbes* 30 Under 30 and honored as Hero
of the Year by Red Bull.

THE ASSEMBLAGE

FROM A YOUNG AGE, I QUESTIONED IF I'LL EVER BE "GOOD ENOUGH."

———————

It's nearly impossible to score a ten out of ten in gymnastics. For a long time, I felt that my enoughness was completely determined by other people and based on the way I look, what I wear, and how I move. Judges critique who you are as a being, and offer a score to reflect that.

By the time I left gymnastics, I was an introverted teenager heading into college. I had spent so much of my life in the gym that I didn't really know how to navigate the real world. My social skills were stunted. In gymnastics and in school, people tell you what to do, and I've always been the type who was good at following instructions. But now it was up to me. I went through seven or eight different majors trying to find my next fire. I didn't know what I wanted for my life, and that was very disorienting.

After college, I spent years going from job to job. First, I did a research fellowship in China for a year. Then I accepted a finance job on Wall Street before taking the leap into entrepreneurship. When fundraising for my first startup, I found myself dealing with challenges that a lot of other female entrepreneurs faced. The venture capital landscape is 94 percent male. An unconscious bias seemed to persist. For example, women are asked different questions from men—what we call "prevention" versus "promotion" questions. A woman might get asked, "What prevents someone from copying you?" whereas a guy might get asked, "Tell me your milestones."

Having had my fair share of those types of experiences, I really wanted to embrace a community of other female entrepreneurs who were also on this journey.

I quickly discovered that there were a lot of women seeking to defy the odds in entreprenuership.

I launched SheWorx thinking it could be a safe place for me to build my business, and it evolved into a global platform for any woman who wanted to launch, fundraise, and scale.

In the beginning, SheWorx was focused on bringing in investors and mentors to discuss specialized topics, host active discussions, and connect female founders with funding. The consistency and quality of these discussions brought in higher and higher caliber investors, which helped SheWorx grow into a global investment platform.

One female entrepreneur attended a SheWorx summit after getting over two hundred rejections. She was trying to raise her first million dollars to build a tech platform for nonprofits. Every single card was stacked against her: she was one of three female founders, a first-time founder, and part of the LGBT community. At the summit, we put her at a table with someone who ended up becoming her first and lead investor for a $1 million seed round. Seeing her close an investor after facing months and months of rejection made me realize that I could actually play an instrumental part in changing the business landscape.

As SheWorx grew, every external indicator said I was on the right path. But deep down, I still lacked confidence. I still never felt like I had done enough.

Like in gymnastics, I sometimes felt as if I was putting on a show for other people. I didn't have the confidence inside that people expected, and I thought that meant something was wrong with me. At the core of my ambition was insecurity.

I feared things I couldn't control, and control is huge for people who want a lot. I could control my body, my performance, and how much work I put in . . . but I couldn't control what others thought of me.

When I turned thirty, I started asking myself, "To what end? To what end am I pursuing more money? More recognition? More titles?" I realized that none of these things made me feel truly fulfilled and happy because enoughness starts with self-acceptance, not external achievement.

It's also about surrounding myself with amazing friends and family who are always there for me.

I've invested more in these relationships in recent times than I have in a long time, and I've learned that being around people who love you for you—not for your achievements—is enough. Having the courage to pursue mastery in one thing—rather than chasing after short-term validation—is fulfillment.

Now I am asked questions like, "When are you getting married? When are you having kids? Are you going to freeze your eggs?" I used to let these questions affect me. They reminded me so viscerally of the pressure I felt growing up. I used to internalize every external pressure and make it about me—my *enoughness*.

Now I choose what I internalize. I've worked hard to get over this need for more and learned to just *be* with my purpose and passion.

I may not be in control of how others see me, but I am in control of how I see myself. When you go into a situation with fear, insecurity, and doubt—it shows.

And when you value how you see yourself, it impacts how others perceive you too. Whether you realize it or not, you have the power to detach from their opinions—to decide it's not about you—to decide that you are enough.

IN A WORLD THAT
FEEDS OFF YOUR
INSECURITY,
LOVING YOURSELF
IS AN ACT OF
REBELLION.

Lisa Carmen Wang

—————

YOU MAY HAVE TO FIGHT A BATTLE MORE THAN ONCE TO WIN IT.

Margaret Thatcher

resilience

GEORGIA
CLARK

Georgia Clark is a novelist, event host, and playwright. She is the author of the critically acclaimed books *The Bucket List, The Regulars,* and *It Had to Be You.* Georgia has also worked as a freelance journalist. Her articles have been published in magazines such as *Cosmopolitan, Cleo, Daily Life, Sunday Life,* and more. In 2017, Georgia founded Generation Women, a monthly storytelling event in the Lower East Side that invites women in their 20s, 30s, 40s, 50s, 60s, and 70s to tell an original story on a theme. Generation Women's mission is to defy stereotypes by bringing women of all ages together and celebrating the fact that we never stop exploring, cultivating, and evolving.

BROOKLYN

I HAD A LITTLE BIT OF SAVINGS AND A DESIRE TO LIVE IN NEW YORK CITY.

———

I moved here in March 2009. It was really cold. Coming from Sydney, I wasn't used to bad weather. I didn't have a cell phone. I didn't know anyone. I didn't have a visa—I didn't know how to get a visa. I didn't even have a job.

Australians love to travel. In my twenties, I traveled to Mexico, around Europe, and across Asia. But it never crossed my mind that I would go to New York City. That seemed as glamorous and exotic as going to the moon.

One day in my late twenties, my roommate in Sydney planned a trip to New York City and invited me along. At the time, it seemed so foreign and far away. New York was literally on the other side of the planet from where I lived and grew up. But as soon as I landed, I had this feeling that I think a lot of people experience when they first arrive—the city was really exciting and so different from anywhere else. We were going out, shopping, drinking, partying, and discovering endlessly. It was the most amazing ten-day trip, and I just fell in love with Brooklyn.

When I returned to Sydney, I started telling everyone that I was moving to New York City. I didn't actually know when or how. Then, on a whim, I entered a competition pitching ideas for television and scripts—and I won. The prize was a round-trip flight to anywhere in the world that would benefit my career, plus a little bit of cash.

There was my ticket back to New York City.

But I didn't end up taking the return flight. I stayed. And a year later, the thrill of moving to the new city billowed and peaked. I was settling into reality. I had written a book but it didn't sell. I couldn't get a job because it was the thick of the Great Recession. I was totally broke. I couldn't even afford the plane ticket home. My parents didn't have any money and had separated, so I couldn't move home with them. I felt so far from my dreams. There was no backup plan.

| The creative life is full of risks, and I had taken a big one that didn't seem like it would ever pay off.

My back was against the wall. I could no longer sustain myself emotionally, psychologically, or financially. By that point, I had been writing books for years and I just wasn't making any money. I took the failure really hard. It was devastating. I needed to see my hard work pay off.

I remember coming across a story that Ellen DeGeneres shares about her lowest point. She was twenty years old and living in a basement apartment. Her girlfriend had just died in a car accident. At her lowest of lows, Ellen declared, "I'm going to be the first female comic that Johnny Carson invites to the couch." At that time, it was a totally ludicrous idea. She wasn't even a comedian. She didn't have a following. But then it happened for her: she was the first female comedian that Johnny Carson invited to the couch.

Being intentional about what you want, even if it sounds like you're overshooting, is really powerful. If you don't articulate what you want, the universe can't make it happen. When I set out to write *The Regulars*, I had a specific agenda to write a bigger book that would be published by a "Big 5" publisher. I also wanted a six-figure advance that would justify the amount of work I put in. Something that would take me up a level. I asked my agent and every writer in my network, "How do I get there? What does this book need to do?"

Articulating my dream meant that the people and events around me could start formulating to make it happen. And it did. *The Regulars* sold for the amount of money I wanted.

It became my first step into the real publishing world. When I received the final version, I held the book in my hands so tightly and started to cry. I couldn't believe it had finally happened. The creative life is so full of failure—so many missteps and projects unrealized. To finally have something work out the way I'd wanted felt incredible. I used to think the worst thing that could happen to me is that I'd write a whole book and it wouldn't sell to a publisher. I've actually done that twice now.

| Successful people are, first and foremost, resilient. They pick themselves back up, keep going, and don't let necessary failures slow them down too much or for too long.

If you need to fall apart, then absolutely, fall apart. In some ways, it's good for you. Then pull yourself back together and get some perspective: fresh air, exercise, and time with friends—they really do help. You realize that life goes on.

A mentor once said to me, "Life is long." And I said, "Really? I thought life was short."

The reality is that you can be creating and working well into your seventies and beyond. Even if things don't work out this month or this year, you have time—and your resilience will be rewarded.

THERE'S NO SUCH THING AS AN OVERNIGHT SUCCESS.

Some people might seem like one because you haven't heard of them before. But in reality, they've been working many years for their moment.

Georgia Clark

THE MOST
DANGEROUS PHRASE
IN THE LANGUAGE
IS, 'WE'VE ALWAYS
DONE IT THIS WAY.'

Grace Hopper

fierce

NATHALIE
MOLINA
NIÑO

Nathalie Molina Niño is an investor (builde
capitalist), serial entrepreneur, and author of *Leapfro*
The New Revolution for Women Entrepreneurs. She i
the cofounder and managing director of Know
Holdings, a financial services platform built t
support a multi-trillion-dollar economy drive
by communities of color. Nathalie is also th
co-founder of Entrepreneurs a Athena at the Athen
Center for Leadership Studies at Barnard Colleg
at Columbia University and has advised industr
leaders ranging from Goldman Sachs, Disney, an
Microsoft to nonprofits such as the Bill & Melind
Gates Foundation, Accion Opportunity Fund, an
the National Institute for Reproductive Health. I
2019, she was honored with the Schneps inaugura
Women of Wall Street Award for her influence i
banking and finance and was named among *Peopl*
magazine's 2019 Most Powerful Latinas.

BARNARD COLLEGE

RUNNING A COMPANY REVEALED BOTH THE BEST AND WORST IN ME.

———————

I t was 2002. I had enough. I told my colleagues and business partners not to call me for a year. I needed to recover.

The dot-com crash had just blown up a successful software localization company I worked tirelessly to build. I had to fire employees in sixteen countries. Literally, I went from country to country, looking people in the face and firing them. It was among the worst experiences in my life. It's one thing to see your business fail and another to take a global tour, rubbing the failure in your own face and the faces of three hundred employees who were already struggling.

I was twenty-six.

I had partnered with the oldest publicly traded company in the US, and it embodied a legacy culture to the core. There were no women at the executive level. All the big-boy deals were made at the golf course. It was just a cutthroat and toxic culture. The office enforced a strict dress code and office hours. Meanwhile, the employees I had brought into the business were a bunch of Internet geeks who came to work in flip-flops and shaggy hair. I didn't care. None of us did.

I spent half of my time and energy protecting my employees from the environment at the parent company. In some ways, you could say the dot-com crash was a blessing, but it certainly didn't feel like it then. The experience transformed how I viewed the world of business.

For a change of pace, I went to my family's ancestral home in Ecuador, where I could just sit around, read books and babysit my niece every afternoon. I didn't want to see or even talk about work, but eleven months into my sabbatical, my business partner called and said, "I need you back." He wanted me to join him in building a new business. I told him my conditions for returning: there would be women at the top and I would have freedom in dictating the culture.

At this new venture, I was immediately parachuted into a crisis situation. Our largest customer was ready to sue us over a failed project. I worked my new team to the bone, and after a number of months, we miraculously turned it around. In fact, we were in the office celebrating when the person who was supposed to deliver the final project files suddenly called in sick. I was stunned. We had worked way too hard to go down like this.

I had my driver go to this employee's home and bring him in by whatever means necessary. When he finally showed up, I made sure he not only started the file transfer but also taught three other people how to do it. The next morning, I was congratulating my team when I heard a knock. "Nathalie, Steven called out sick again—" I cut her off: "Who cares? We now have three other people who know how to deliver the files." She caught her breath and finished, "Steven is at the hospital in the cardiac ward."

> In the eyes of the company, we had saved the day. We delivered the project and averted a business disaster. But I consider this crisis among my greatest failures.

At that moment, I thought of my immigrant parents, who raised me to say "please" and "thank you" and to be kind, and it all hit me—I had completely lost my way.

I thought I was different from the horrific culture that I'd desperately tried to escape, but I ended up doing the same that I judged them for: putting profit above the life of a human being.

I left the office that morning and walked around Dublin until nightfall, thinking hard about what I had become.

At what point did the road fork?

I wish I could say that I woke up the next day and became this wonderful manager and fabulous human, but the truth is, it's taken me years to find my way again. The shadow side is always there.

In 2013, I cofounded a center for women entrepreneurs at Barnard College. There, I worked with brilliant young women who started asking me to help them get into tech.

But this was an industry that I'd fled. . . . Was I supposed to just feed these girls to the lions? It weighed on me that I'd left the industry after fifteen years in no better shape than I'd found it. I had only cared about winning, not changing it or paying it forward.

> If you had asked me back then, "Why aren't you more of an activist?" I would've told you that I can only do one thing at a time: I can make my company thrive so I can make sure my employees have jobs, or I can be an activist. But that's bullshit.

Now that I am an investor, I'm in a position to prove it and be a part of the movement. In 2016, I started BRAVA Investments to back businesses that have the potential to raise up and improve the lives of millions of women, like a company making the birth control pill available over-the-counter for the first time in history. And this year, I'm launching my next venture, Known. It is centered around ownership for communities of color and the economy we power, but don't own.

> Until we prove that investments in Black, Indigenous, and other minoritized people of color are lucrative, people will always think of it as a charitable act or niche investment with lower returns.

People of color are 70 percent of the world's population and yet we control less than 2 percent of global capital—we're *not* a niche. It's time we take the driver's seat in the global economy.

I am amazed that life has now taken me full circle—to build a business for both profit and people.

I WAS THE ONLY WOMAN IN THE ROOM FOR MOST OF MY CAREER.

You can walk away from an experience like that traumatized or you can walk away excited about fixing it.

Nathalie Molina Niño

I'D RATHER REGRET THE THINGS THAT I HAVE DONE THAN THE THINGS THAT I HAVE NOT DONE.

Lucille Ball

audacious

MAHOGANY
L. BROWNE

Mahogany L. Browne is a renowned poet, writer, educator, and organizer. She is known for poetry that challenges society's stereotypes of Black women. Among Mahogany's notable works is "Black Girl Magic," a poem that has become an anthem for Black female empowerment under the movement #BlackGirlMagic and celebrated for its significant feminist content by the Amelia Bloomer Book List in 2019. Dazed Digital declared *Black Girl Magic*, an anthology of Black women poets, co-edited by Mahogany, as "one of the most important volumes of poetry in recent years." Mahogany has been featured on *PBS NewsHour*, HBO's *Brave New Voices*, and other global platforms. In July 2021, she was named the first ever poet-in-residence at New York City's Lincoln Center.

BROOKLYN

A SEVEN-YEAR-OLD GIRL MEMORIZED "BLACK GIRL MAGIC."

———

She performed it at an oratory competition. And let me tell you—I had no idea I could cry so much. I can't put my finger on who exactly I've had the most impact on, but I can tell you who's had the greatest impact on me.

Seeing that young person perform a poem that I wrote for women who'd lost a child to police brutality made me realize that my work was becoming a part of an intergenerational discussion.

This little seven-year-old changed my life.

And my life, given the way I grew up, wasn't supposed to look like this. I worked for it, don't get me wrong. . . . But people work hard for their whole lives and still get caught in the statistics of where they come from. It still surprises me that I'm here, considering all the circumstances that almost killed my dreams.

I was raised by a single mother. My father was in prison. I think that's why I became interested in books at such a young age. Each story offered a world where I didn't have to think about where my dad wasn't or why my mom worked so much. That's not to say my mom wasn't supportive—she celebrated us whenever and however she could. Mom was all about us dreaming big because she never got to live out hers.

But then my mom hurt herself at work. The doctors put her on opioids for the pain. Within a year, between her pain and depression, Mom transformed from a doting parent into an addict. Random people started showing up at our home. I was constantly fighting off drug dealers. Then someone stole our car. . . . It was a lot for a seventeen-year-old. It's a lot for anyone. Writing became my escape. It was always the focus of my education, but after my home life spiraled, it became a way for me to preserve the memory of my mom.

After high school, I studied at a community college while working as an editor for a regional hip-hop magazine. As I was transferring into a four-year program at San Francisco State University, I got an opportunity to move to New York City and intern as a writer. It eventually led to a full-time offer from an online hip-hop magazine.

So many people, including my family, told me that this was a horrible idea: "You have a baby. You don't even have a community in New York City. What are you thinking?" Everyone was placing their fears on me.

> But in my mind, everything horrible was already happening. How much worse could it get? I wasn't going to let fear control me.

I was hungry to see outside of my neighborhood. In New York City, I found my calling. I loved hip-hop, and as long as I could write, I was happy. It didn't matter whether it was for a magazine or newspaper.

But the satisfaction was short-lived.

During one assignment, a musician I was interviewing suddenly had a mental breakdown. One minute, we were having a conversation about music, and the next, he snapped and threatened me with a pistol while he was driving us to another space. I immediately jumped out of the car. I said that this interaction was going to be in my piece. I wasn't going to sit there quietly and allow something like this to happen.

But the editors told me I couldn't write about my experience because it would jeopardize the advertising dollars from that artist's label. The closer I got to seeing which stories actually made the page, the more I realized how misogynistic this industry was. Not only did I exit the interview, I needed to leave this environment. It just wasn't worth it anymore.

So I transitioned to poetry and focused there. There was no editor telling me what I could or couldn't say. I had no idea what it took to be a full-time poet. I just knew that writing poems was an offset moment for me. It was like dipping into a different ink. I was my own editor and could write whatever I wanted. At first, I was shunned and ignored. People would say, "I'll pay you because you're cute, but I shouldn't have to pay you this much because you're not *him*."

I found myself susceptible to other people's ideas of me and what I deserved. But I just kept going and pushed past the negativity because I knew I was reaching someone. My community was my barometer. They reminded me that my voice matters. People coming from a place of misogyny have nothing to do with me and they can't stop me from achieving my dreams.

At home, the inequities made me sad. But at work, I was excited to fight for money, respect, and equal time on the stage. I collaborated with other poets, went on tour, wrote chapbooks, and even launched my own publishing imprint. This was back when self-publishing wasn't even a thing. I just had absolutely nothing to lose, so I wrote what I wanted and the world had to hear it.

Then, in 2018, "Black Girl Magic" happened. With amazing editors and an agent behind me, it was the first time I didn't have to fight for money, recognition, or to be heard. I cried when I received my first contract. It's like the universe was saying, "This has been waiting for you this whole time. Here you go."

People doubt themselves as a defense mechanism—a way to prepare for the blow. I won't live like that.

My mom wanted to become a chef. And even though she didn't have the wherewithal to chase her dreams, she showed me what it meant to have them. Her inaction inspired me to do something about mine.

This joy I have could've been the joy she had, always. But my mom didn't have a blueprint for that journey. I also don't think she had the kind of support that I ended up finding, especially in New York City. That's why I strive to be that support system for others.

There are plenty of ways to succeed—to surpass not just your own expectations but also those of others. You just have to find your special sauce. It comes down to the way you do it that will bring you happiness.

YOU HAVE TO TAKE A CHANCE ON YOURSELF. YOU JUST HAVE TO.

Mahogany L. Browne

DWELL IN
POSSIBILITY. FIND
ECSTASY IN LIFE;
THE MERE SENSE
OF LIVING IS JOY
ENOUGH.

Emily Dickinson

nourish

JOAN
FALLON

Dr. Joan Fallon is the founder of Curemark, a revolutionary biopharmaceutical company that is developing new treatments for neurological diseases with limited or unmet needs. As a pediatric physician with over twenty-five years of experience, she was among the first to discover a correlation between the gut and brain that contributes to autism in children. This finding led her and her team at Curemark to develop the drug CM-AT, which received Fast Track status from the FDA.

MIDTOWN

THE BEST GIFT ANYONE HAS GIVEN ME IS A STETHOSCOPE WHEN I WAS TEN.

I'd always known I wanted to be a doctor. I think it came from seeing human beings suffer. I take it all very personally. It's difficult to see things that you either can't help or that should've been helped.

With my parents' encouragement, I went on to become a doctor, and years later, I opened a private practice with a focus on pediatric development. A large part of my work was treating children with autism. Those days, the medical community had little understanding of autism, what caused it or how to treat it. But truthfully, the behavioral treatments alone never made intuitive sense to me. I thought there must be a physiological aspect to the condition.

For example, I was told that kids with autism didn't eat protein because they didn't like the texture of it in their mouths. I thought, "Wait a minute—every child's sensory is different. How could they all have aversion to the same texture?"

I questioned it because I knew the kids. Throughout my years of practice, I had picked up on a pattern in their diets that I believed could play a role in how autism developed in the brain.

I had discovered that autism may have a gut-brain connection.

These were the early days, before microbiomes were well understood. It was before we knew that the gut could affect the brain. For every supporter I had, there were ten on the other side. People bullied me: "Who are you to discover this? Who do you think you are?"

But I knew I was onto something. I also knew I needed to know more. So I went back to school to learn how to do clinical trials. For three years, I was seeing patients, commuting twice a week for school, and writing patents. I gave up my personal time and life as I knew it. I had discovered something with potential, even though I had no idea where it was going.

It became evident that I had to either do something with this discovery, or not.

I knew I had to try. If I tried and I failed, then I tried and I failed. But if I didn't try, I would never be able to help those kids, and I felt it was the most important work I could do with my life.

So I left practice for a new journey as CEO. I gave up my retirement money to write patents. I gave up my relationship. I took a risk. A *big risk*. And I'm glad I did.

In the early days of Curemark, I was so focused on the mission that I didn't have time to entertain doubt. Then, the challenges of starting a company settled in. What am I doing? Am I doing the right thing?

For the first five years, I had nothing but naysayers. On top of that, I had given up a practice where I went into an office and saw people every day. With Curemark, I suddenly had nowhere to go. I was alone. It was very traumatic for me.

What kept me going was a natural drive to do what I wanted to do. When you're younger, you tend to think your worth is in what you achieve. I think everyone goes through that. But I soon learned it's about feeding yourself. It's doing the things you love that nourish your soul.

I'm fanatic about baseball so for me, that meant attending umpire training camp for Major League Baseball. I remember how out of place I felt, running around with 150 young men on those hot summer days.

But the experience brought me out of a grind and created headspace for me to reset and renew.

You have to celebrate the wins, even the little ones. I've watched people fail in their businesses and projects simply because they don't think it's important to set aside time to grow themselves outside of work. Work and life are not two discrete things.

If you don't feed your life, then your work alone will be off balance.

I liken this to the game of whack-a-mole. You hit the mole more accurately if you don't look straight at it. When you focus slightly off-center, your peripheral vision activates your reflexes. This is how life works too. You're more likely to catch signs and seize opportunities when you are nourishing your life as a whole. A narrow focus overlooks the big picture. Cultivate your passions and trust your instincts.

You'll know you're taking the right step if going forward feels rational and going backward feels like succumbing to fear.

That's the instinct I trusted when I gave up twenty-five years of practice. If someone had said to me that I would one day be CEO of a biotech company this far along, I would've said there's no way. I had no idea what that would even look like. But here we are, just a few years from releasing the first treatment for autism to the market.

While I don't have any kids of my own, in a way, I feel like I have thousands of them. This is all for them. The day that families can go to the pharmacy and get this medicine for their kids—that's the day I will get my sense of relief.

THINK OF GOLF.

You have to take everything into
consideration—the wind, the trees,
the grass, the length of your club.
But once you take your swing, you
can't think about anything else.
You just have to go for it.

You have to tune out the noise.
You have to tune out the noise.
You have to tune out the noise.

Joan Fallon

I KNOW THAT, LIKE EVERY WOMAN OF THE PEOPLE, I HAVE MORE STRENGTH THAN I APPEAR TO HAVE.

Evita Perón

determined

MARY
CLAVIERES

Mary Clavieres is the founder and CEO of Brief Transitions, a company providing postpartum mesh underwear to women after childbirth and surgeries. She is also the founder of the Transitions Collective, a community platform that offers support and resources for women who are building businesses and raising families. In addition, Mary provides corporate consulting on leadership, team effectiveness, and change management.

HOBOKEN, NEW JERSEY

I OFTEN WISH I STARTED MY COMPANY EARLIER.

But I also know my business couldn't have existed before I became a mom. Brief Transitions came out of a personal need after the birth of my first daughter. We produce mesh underwear for women after childbirth, particularly C-sections. The underwear is super stretchy, so it doesn't put pressure on the midsection. The hospital sends you home with a few pairs, but not enough. I wanted to make them available on the market for moms like me.

It still seems wild to me that I'm an entrepreneur who left her corporate job. I was in corporate for almost fourteen years. I did well there and I enjoyed what I was doing, but a little voice did creep in along the way: "Should I be doing something else? Is this it? Do you just go on with your nine-to-five and retire?"

After the birth of my daughter, I started to feel the shift more. Even when I first started Brief Transitions, I wasn't intending to leave my corporate job. It was kind of just . . . "Oh, maybe I'll do this and help some moms since I couldn't find the underwear for myself."

It just didn't seem like becoming an entrepreneur would ever be a step for me. And that's because "entrepreneur" wasn't the definition of success I grew up with. Neither of my parents went to college, so they were really focused on having me contribute to the corporate world with the skills I gained through formal education. For a long time, I equated success with climbing the corporate ladder.

And I was, for the most part, happy in the corporate world. But in 2018, I started traveling almost every week for my job. To put it into perspective, I was home for only three weeks that whole first quarter of the year. It became unsustainable. That was not success for me anymore. I had two young daughters who started asking, "Why isn't Mommy home?"

That was the turning point for me.

Over the course of weeks, I kept thinking, "Now is when I'll give my notice to leave." But I ended up prolonging it, telling myself, "Oh, now is not really a good time. Maybe I'll wait a bit longer. . ."

A friend confronted me: "Why? Why did you push it out again?"

I realized I had no real reason except that I was utterly terrified. I just felt so uncomfortable. It took me three or four tries before I actually did it. I was really scared that I would fail. What if Brief Transitions would be a big flop? What if I wouldn't have any customers? Or what if I wouldn't bring in any money? I like being an earner and contributing to the family, and I was scared that I wouldn't be able to do that anymore. My job had been part of my identity for so many years.

> Launching Brief Transtions felt like jumping out of a plane without a safety net. The entire process of building in this way requires a different mindset.

I started with a goal of selling only forty units a month, and it took me a while to even get there. But once I hit selling forty units in one day, I realized that Brief Transitions really could be something on its own. That gave me so much hope because I realized that if I could do it once, I could do it again. Now I'm selling hundreds of units each month.

Breaking through my fear has given me confidence I never had before.

Some women fear that being a mother or entrepreneur means having to choose one path or the other, and I can understand why.

For mom entrepreneurs, the biggest struggle is time—having that quality time to spend with your kids but also with your business because a business is your baby too.

But I think you can be a better mom because you work. Even though I'm not traveling anymore, I'm still not home every moment of the day. But when I am, I make it count. When my older daughter asks, "Are you going on another trip?" I can now say, "No, I'm finished with those."

I try to incorporate my mission into something meaningful to my girls. I explain what my business is, why I'm in it, and I tell them about the incredible entrepreneurs in the Transitions Collective—a community of women and moms I formed to empower one another on this journey.

> It's a big part of being successful—having other people around you who support you. It will elevate you so much.

Life is a balancing act every day and some days are just exhausting. But I'm driven by a purpose beyond that of just being a mom, entrepreneur, or wife.

I want to set an example for my two girls that they can do anything they put their minds to. I want them to grow up seeing Mom as a doer, as someone who's really hardworking and willing to put in the time. I hope to show them that they don't have to settle or be okay with something they're not happy with.

More than anything, I want to show them courage. It takes a lot to do this. But once you do the thing you built up in your mind to be the hardest, the possibilities become wide open.

BECOMING A MOM IS WHAT ALLOWED ME TO TAKE UNIMAGINABLE LEAPS TODAY.

As women, we are incredibly capable in
every phase of our lives.

Mary Clavieres

WHEN I DARE TO
BE POWERFUL—TO
USE MY STRENGTH
IN THE SERVICE OF
MY VISION—THEN IT
BECOMES LESS AND
LESS IMPORTANT
WHETHER I AM
AFRAID.

Audre Lorde

courage

VALERIE
WEISLER

Valerie Weisler is the founder and CEO of the Validation Project, a nonprofit organization that works with more than six thousand teenagers in 105 countries on social justice projects to combat bullying. She is a graduate of Muhlenberg College, where she studied education advocacy. Valerie has been internationally recognized with accolades such as the National Jefferson Award for Peace and Justice and the Diana Award from former UK prime minister, David Cameron. She speaks on behalf of the US Department of State on topics such as the inequalities in education and the importance of positive learning environments.

GRAND CENTRAL STATION

MY PARENTS' DIVORCE CHANGED ME OVERNIGHT.

———————

Just a few days before my first year of high school, my parents announced their plan to separate. That conversation shattered my world. I thought that it might have been something I said that made them not love each other anymore.

I suddenly transformed from happy-go-lucky Val into someone who was terrified of saying anything. In fact, I made it a game: How long could I go without looking at anyone or talking?

Silence was my safety blanket. I thought that if I didn't do or say anything, then I couldn't hurt others, and they couldn't hurt me.

I was wrong.

The kids at school noticed. "Do you not have the physical ability to talk? Are you actually mute?" A group of girls bombarded my locker with notes saying that I shouldn't bother coming to school if I wasn't going to speak. I crouched farther and farther down in class, hiding in my baggy sweats. But the more I hoped to go unnoticed, the more of a target I became.

The bullying was so terrible at times that I dreaded waking up in the morning. I felt lifeless. There seemed to be no light at the end of the tunnel.

I was lucky to have my mom, but everything else was dark. I felt so isolated, while everyone around me was having this seemingly amazing high school experience.

Then one day, I saw a classmate at his locker—surrounded by other students who were tormenting him for being overweight. He took it silently, unable to lift his head. I felt his pain. It was the first time I realized this was not just happening to me, but all around me.

I approached him and said what I had wanted someone to say to me all along: "You matter. I'm going through the same thing and I want you to know that you're not alone."

His reaction shocked me. He shared that he had been planning to take his own life later that day. He was not only bullied at school but also at home. No part of his life felt safe. He said that my words validated him—that I saved his life.

Validation. That word lit a fire in me.

Validating people—helping them recognize that they matter—could be a solution to bullying. From the moment I reached home from school that day to the moment my mom made me go to bed, I thought about how to create a safe community for teens to come together and focus on the positive.

I named it the Validation Project and launched a website. That first version was neon pink with Comic Sans font and fuzzy clip art. It wasn't my best work but it was a start.

The initiative began as an intimate lunch group with a few classmates and me sharing our struggles. Then, other students caught on and began emailing me about their experiences of being bullied. It was like the Validation Project had become their trusted confidant and outlet. As the number of stories grew, the local news picked up on my work, and I started hearing from students in other states and, eventually, other countries.

Every person who came forward with a story of struggle also shared what was saving them each day. It was their passion—playing an instrument, working with a community organization, or writing, for example.

Anti-bullying is by nature a reactive response.

The victim is already damaged. I wanted to see if bullying could be prevented by empowering students to use their passions to proactively solve community problems and build their self-confidence at the same time. After all, founding the Validation Project was what helped me overcome my own depression.

> As the Validation Project grew, the media wanted to know more about the fifteen-year-old girl behind the vision. I suddenly had to put my struggles into words. I was forced to find my voice.

Finding that voice put me on a path of having to figure out more than just bullying.

I am gay.

I have probably known that since I was five years old. But as the Validation Project grew, I was still hiding that part of myself, telling people to take pride in who they were while I was putting on a mask every day. When the Validation Project received an award from GLSEN (the Gay, Lesbian, and Straight Education Network), I decided to share in my speech that I was a part of this community. Putting it out there felt so scary but also invigorating. In revealing my true self, I was representing teenagers around the world who didn't have the opportunity to share their truths.

Despite my accomplishments, the young, scared Val still emerges in moments of insecurity. Her voice likes to sneak in: "Maybe I shouldn't be talking to this CEO or speaking at such a high-profile event. Who am I to do this?"

Pushing that voice away means I am simply extending the deadline to deal with my own self-doubt. Confronting it is accepting an important truth: the struggles you've been through in your past and who you are today are the same person. And that's okay. For me, both versions living side by side is the reason the Validation Project came to be. For you, both versions side by side define the unique purpose that you are meant to fill.

I SUBCONSCIOUSLY INSERTED MYSELF INTO A POSITION OF LEADERSHIP.

I signed my emails as 'CEO,' and for a long time, I didn't even know what that meant. But now I know that it stood for a change. I was empowering students to stand against bullying.

Students like me.

Valerie Weisler

WE MUST HAVE PERSEVERANCE AND ABOVE ALL CONFIDENCE IN OURSELVES. WE MUST BELIEVE THAT WE ARE GIFTED FOR SOMETHING AND THAT THIS THING MUST BE ATTAINED.

Marie Curie

daring

PALAK
PATEL

Palak Patel is a chef at the Institute of Culinary
Education and owner of Dash + Chutney, an Indian
street food eatery in Atlanta, GA. She is also an
award-winning celebrity chef and TV personality.
Palak began moonlighting as a personal chef in
2006 and later earned a culinary degree from the
prominent International Culinary Center in New
York. She gained national recognition after being
featured on *Chopped*, *Beat Bobby Flay*, and other Food
Network programs. Palak has been recognized on
the *Today Show* and in media publications including
Forbes, *Thrive Global*, *Mashable*, and *Marie Claire*.
With a mission to bring joy through food, Palak
has a global cooking style influenced by her Indian
heritage and her travels to over fifty countries.

PALAK'S KITCHEN

SIMPLY HEARING THAT YOU SHOULD PURSUE YOUR PASSION DOESN'T MEAN MUCH.

———

I'm not saying you shouldn't. But the passion has to be so alive that you'd be willing to do whatever it takes. And if you are deeply in love with your work, then the path will find you.

I found that magic in India, where I grew up living with my extended family of fifteen in a three-story house. Back then, a meal for fifteen wasn't uncommon, and since we didn't have a refrigerator, there was no concept of leftovers. It was a remarkable time and it instilled in me this notion of eating together, cooking together, and being together.

I must've been just four or five years-old when I started trying simple recipes. My mom said I would beg her to let me do even the littlest things, like make chai for guests. I just naturally gravitated toward cooking. I wanted to figure things out.

The first time I became drawn to doing this as a career was a few years out of undergrad. I was working in a corporate job in Atlanta when I began exploring Le Cordon Bleu's culinary program just for fun. I went in for an orientation and then tried speaking to my parents about it.

But before I could even finish my sentence, their answer was no.

Like most immigrant daughters, I stayed on the career path that my parents envisioned for me: the *safe* path.

Shortly after, I moved to San Francisco. I figured it was a great culinary city and it would be the farthest from my parents. I'd have more freedom to just learn. I can't tell you how much learning and discovering I experienced just by virtue of living there. Wine country was right around the corner. Every single meal was heaven. Even going to the farmer's market was something new.

At the height of my exploration, I came across an organization that trained and certified personal chefs. I thought, "Since my parents don't want me to quit my corporate job, I'll just start my own little business on the side." I didn't even tell my parents at first, but then I started making $1,000 to cook dinner for just four people. My parents were stunned—it was really good money for a side hustle.

At one of these gigs, I met a CEO. He said, "I didn't know you had a degree in business. Come work for me at my startup." On paper, it looked like I was swapping one corporate job for another, but now I had a chance to marry both of my worlds. The new job required me to travel, and I explored amazing countries like China, Taiwan, the Philippines, and Japan, just eating my way around. It was a beautiful, parallel path.

But deep down, I still wasn't really happy in my day job. The only thing that made it palatable was the incredible travel and food. Eventually, I took a relocation to New York City and enrolled in culinary school as a thirty-first birthday gift to myself. I went to classes at night so that it wouldn't interfere with my corporate job.

Even after I landed on the radar of *Chopped* and the Food Network, my coworkers had no idea about my side gig. People in meetings would be like, "I know you from somewhere! Where do I know you from?" I'd win *Beat Bobby Flay* on TV, then come into the office the next day like nothing happened. How wild is that?!

Living in two worlds was exhausting. At one point, I remember hoping I'd get sick just so that I wouldn't have to go into the office. It was *that* unbearable. Yet I still wasn't ready to give up the financial attachments, my parents' expectations, and a vision of what I thought my life should be.

I'd question myself: "Who am I to make money doing what I love? What makes me good enough?"

Then in 2015, I lost a seven-figure deal for the startup. The writing was on the wall. My boss, who now knew about my not-so-secret side job, encouraged me to just take the exit package and go cook.

In hindsight, I wish I'd quit sooner. But fear held me back so much. Even after I quit, I didn't have the courage to articulate my dreams. The first year was just focused on survival. *How do I make enough money to stay afloat?* I took every gig that came because I didn't want to take a financial hit.

But the more projects I pursued, the more confident I became. Experience helped me anticipate hiccups. While it's true I hadn't worked my way up as a line cook, my corporate background taught me how to run a business, manage P&L, and pitch new opportunities. The quicker I pushed through my firsts, the more easily I could move forward.

Now in my forties, I'm beginning to understand why choosing this path was so complicated.

I've ripped open my life in therapy to recognize how my upbringing and childhood programmed me to avoid risks and ignore my true calling. It now goes back to a simple truth: *I love cooking.* How can I amplify that? My intention is to bring joy through food, and that can happen in so many ways. For example, I am opening a plant-based Indian street food concept called Dash + Chutney in a food hall of my hometown in Atlanta, GA. I'm also launching food products and online cooking courses. Life is full of opportunity. I just needed to show up and say yes.

You don't have to get stuck on how everything is going to happen or how you'll make money. Just take the next step. Serendipitously, conversations start to happen and the right people start showing up. The only difference between you and someone building something similar is that they did it.

They got out of their own way.

THE BIGGEST CHALLENGE IS REFRAMING YOUR MINDSET.

Stop focusing on skills and resources you *don't* have and capitalize on what you do have.

Palak Patel

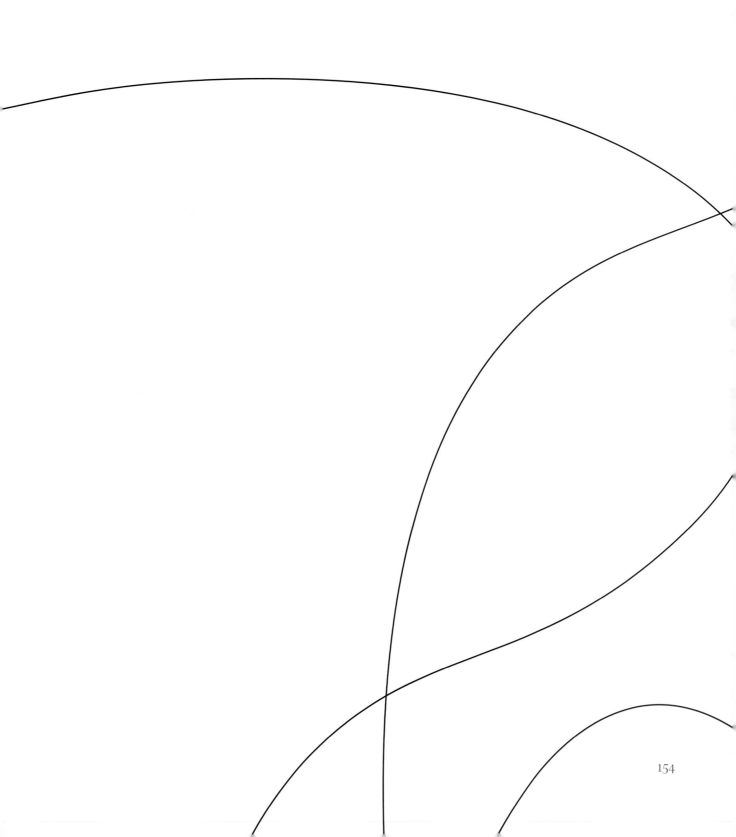

154

I HAVE LEARNED OVER THE YEARS THAT WHEN ONE'S MIND IS MADE UP, THIS DIMINISHES FEAR; KNOWING WHAT MUST BE DONE DOES AWAY WITH FEAR.

Rosa Parks

grit

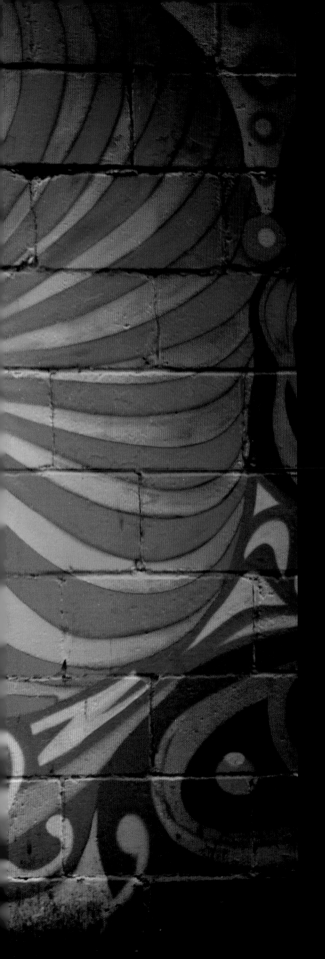

TELISA
DAUGHTRY

TeLisa Daughtry is a social entrepreneur and technology advocate for women and girls around the world. She is the creator of FlyTechnista, a mobile app that provides women and girls with access to curated education, employment, and entrepreneurship opportunities in technology. TeLisa is also an active investor in female founders and has spoken about entrepreneurship for the White House, the UN, SXSW, and more.

LOWER EAST SIDE

I LIVED ON THE TRAIN
FOR SIX MONTHS.

The E train. I was *homeless*. I intentionally chose the E train because it was kind of warm, and when I was cold, it was one of the longest routes I could spend underground. I would ride it from Jamaica Center down to 14th Street.

People think that homelessness happens because of substance abuse or money mismanagement. I never once thought that I could be in that situation. In fact, I could have easily gone home. I have a family. I don't have any issues there. However, my own stubbornness to stay in New York City kept me here almost dangerously longer than I needed to be.

Coming out of college and moving to the city for the first time, young people have these dreams. I was one of those *dreamers*. I had this amazing job creating motion graphics, but the company went under when Wall Street collapsed in 2008. Out of nowhere, I was jobless and, eventually, homeless.

But I remained determined to see my dreams through. I think it stemmed from a passion that was always there. As a child growing up in Boston, I was part of the first enrolling class at Boston Arts Academy, which is a school for visual and performing arts. I was originally enrolled in dance, but it was their visual arts program that appealed to me. Here, I was exposed to creating art with technology for the first time.

Until then, I had seen myself only as a fine artist or a dancer. The program opened up my mind to learn that I could make digital art and also put it up online.

Back then, you couldn't just easily upload and share. You needed to know programming. This was 1998, when there were no coding initiatives—no Girls Who Code. I didn't even have a computer at home. But once I knew this was what I needed to do, I went to Barnes & Noble literally every day after school to hand-copy code because I didn't have money to buy the books.

> Once the door opened for me, I couldn't see myself wanting to do anything else. I didn't want to go back to dancing. I didn't want to do anything but create and use technology to do it.

The problem was, I didn't know that programming could be a real career. My mom was a single mom working four jobs to provide for us. I just wanted to make quick money. So, I quietly dropped out senior year of high school.

Then I saw my friends walk across the stage. And I felt stupid. My mom's greatest hope for me was to graduate because she never did. We were now five generations of no one attending college or having a professional career.

I didn't want to let her down.

A year later, I received my GED and went on to graduate with a bachelor's degree in interactive media design from The New England Institute of Art. In college, I landed an internship at Viacom doing motion graphics for ESPN.

I loved it. And I excelled at it. They offered me full-time opportunities with MTV in the city . . . and that's what brought me here.

> Just taking the bold action of pursuing my own journey opened the door for my relatives to do it after me, because they'd never seen anyone do it.

Just a few years into my dream career, I found myself suddenly jobless and then homeless during the Great Recession. It broke me. I was so scared.

I didn't want to tell people. I didn't want my family to find out and force me back to Boston. New York City meant everything to me.

I began searching for the next thing that could allow me to stay. I freelanced using the Wi-Fi at Starbucks until it closed and then went back to the E train every night with my blue suitcase.

I advocated for myself, interviewing left and right. It was such a humbling experience. Six months went by. When I didn't even have enough money to get back on the train, the phone rang. *It was a job offer.*

Here's the thing about New York: you wait, and wait, and sometimes wait even longer for the opportunity to "make it." Once I jumped back on my feet, I knew I wanted to help others looking for that start.

Navigating a technology career in corporate America as a Black woman wasn't easy. I questioned myself a lot—my abilities . . . my mission. But then I'd think about all the women and girls I'd be letting down. Who was going to care about their journeys as much as I did?

I had to push past my imposter syndrome in order to build FlyTechnista. And it was so worth it. Since launching in 2015, we've helped over eight thousand women and girls get access to education and careers in technology.

Looking forward, I don't always know what my next step is or whether it will be better than the one before. The truth is, no one really does.

I just want people to know the journey that awaits you won't always be easy. But always keep your joy, your passion, your creativity, your curiosity, and your fearlessness.

Go shatter that glass ceiling.

NEVER LET YOUR HARDSHIPS DEFINE YOU.

They will refine you—like the process
of alchemy. Emerging from the fire,
you will shine like pure gold.

TeLisa Daughtry

SOMEONE I ONCE
LOVED GAVE ME
A BOX FULL OF
DARKNESS. IT
TOOK ME YEARS
TO UNDERSTAND
THAT THIS, TOO,
WAS A GIFT.

Maya Angelou

authentic

TIFFANY *PHAM*

Tiffany Pham is an entrepreneur, author, and TV personality. She is the founder and CEO of Mogul, one of the largest digital platforms for diverse talent in the world, empowering others to reach their highest potential through curated job opportunities, education, and events. Mogul has been recognized by *Forbes, Entrepreneur,* and more. Tiffany was a judge on the TLC show *Girl Starter,* a *Forbes* 30 Under 30 honoree, and one of *ELLE* magazine's Women Who Are Changing the World. She is the author of *Girl Mogul* and *You Are a Mogul,* a national bestseller and ranked among the top ten bestselling business books by the *Wall Street Journal.*

MOGUL HQ, UNION SQUARE

I'LL ADMIT I USED TO BE VERY RIGID ABOUT MY LIFE TIMELINES.

———

B ack in college, I went through a phase of studying averages. I thought that based on when the vast majority of people were hitting life's key milestones, I should be getting married by twenty-eight and having kids by thirty. But once I graduated, that timeline completely flew out the window.

The week I launched Mogul was also the week my boyfriend of three years and I broke up. It left me brokenhearted at a time that should've been the highlight of my life. In hindsight, I should've seen it coming. Over the course of our three years together, of all the main hustles and side hustles I had going on, being his girlfriend was the toughest job.

In the beginning, he swept me off my feet. He was smart, ambitious, and charming, and we seemed to share a future vision for a marriage of equals—two people with equal responsibilities and supporting each other's dreams and careers. But as time passed, things started to change. He grew increasingly focused on winning—and on proving he was better, smarter, and stronger than me. He began taunting my shortcomings, teasing me in front of friends, and downplaying my achievements.

Finally, he confessed that what he wanted in a partner had changed. He now wanted someone who would be content in a more traditional role—someone who would be happy staying home, cooking, and doing the dishes. He then asked me to choose: him or Mogul.

It is easier to follow the more traditional path—to give up your dreams and live by timelines set by others.

What changed in our relationship? I think he stopped chasing his dreams. Maybe he expected me to be more like him.

When we first met, he was passionate about writing and dreamed of being a comedy writer someday. But then he worried that writing wouldn't be lucrative enough. At least not immediately. So he gave up the dream and went into finance. Looking back, I don't think he was angry at me for what I was doing with my life. I think he was angry at himself for what he wasn't doing with his.

Pursuing your own path may be harder, but it's far more rewarding because each step you take is built on the step you took before.

Even though it can be hard to ignore the success that others seem to easily achieve by taking the road more traveled, don't look at them to determine your own path forward.

You probably have multiple passions, and that's okay. Your "why" can evolve from a broad purpose to a narrower path that gets you to a totally different place from where you started—that's all part of the journey.

When I was graduating from business school, most of my friends were going into either investment banking or consulting, but I didn't want to follow the herd.

Instead I was interested in creating an impact on people's access to information and opportunity, so I worked in media and entertainment. I later focused further on providing job opportunities and training by pursuing my passion for empowering every person to become the best version of themselves—and that's what led to me creating Mogul.

Choosing Mogul over my relationship was hard—and really, really painful. But it also meant that I would be free to own my ambition, chase my dreams, and not minimize myself in order to soothe someone else's ego. I needed to let go of expectations for when certain milestones should happen, and be open to new possibilities—including a partner who supports my passions and a thriving future for Mogul. It's not easy, but if we collectively stop comparing our lives to others, we could develop more authentic expectations for ourselves.

Each one of us needs to start that trend. If you're not already a part of it, you need to be because it's a relief once you are. Stop looking at other people's social media. Limit what you know about what other people are accomplishing.

You can let go of internal expectations through external actions. The best way to tune out the noise is to stay focused on what you're doing and why you're doing it. With momentum behind you, it'll become easier and easier to tune everything else out.

Throughout my twenties, I had enough passion for my "why" to push myself to work through the night. It always felt right, even though I had no idea whether I would find success.

There was no doubt in my mind that I had to do these things and learn as quickly as possible. The more I poured myself into the process, the more interesting opportunities I received.

The best way to overcome self-doubt is to act. You can alleviate anxiety over the unknowns with action—email clients, call mentors, and get the right resources in place.

Keep going—keep striving. With each success, you will find more courage to stay on your path. At the end of the day, what's most important is where you are now. Concentrate on what you hope to achieve for the world— for your community and for your family.

It will give you clarity on your "why," and the boldness to pursue it.

FOCUS ON RELEASING YOUR EXPECTATIONS.

Your age does not determine if you'll find what you're looking for. It's your state of mind that determines if you are ready for it to come into your life.

Tiffany Pham

JUST DON'T GIVE UP TRYING TO DO WHAT YOU REALLY WANT TO DO. WHERE THERE IS LOVE AND INSPIRATION, I DON'T THINK YOU CAN GO WRONG.

Ella Fitzgerald

liberation

JOCELYN
AREM

Jocelyn Arem is a singer-songwriter who goes by the stage name Rabasi Joss. She is a Grammy Award-nominated archival storytelling producer and founder of Arbo Radiko, a production studio that transforms archival content into modern-day multimedia documentary projects. Her internationally acclaimed work reimagines creative legacies.

STUDIO E, BROOKLYN

I GREW UP IN THE WOODS. I'VE ALWAYS FELT CONNECTED TO TREES.

To me, branches on a tree represent the past and present intertwined. That's the idea behind Arbo Radiko, the production company I founded. Arbo Radiko means "Tree Root" in Esperanto. Our mission is to transform historically significant archival content into modern-day multimedia projects that shine a light on hidden voices and forge a more inclusive future.

I come from Maryland but my roots are in New York. I feel more at home in New York City than any other place I've lived. There is an energy in this city, amplified by the transience of other artists, that makes me feel honed into my craft.

I've always been a musician at heart, so falling into the music business was a natural extension of staying as close to music as possible. I started performing when I was eighteen at this tiny coffee shop called Caffè Lena in Saratoga Springs. But just making music there didn't feel like enough. Caffè Lena has been around since the 1960s. It's the oldest continuously running folk music venue in the US, with a rich legacy of performers. I didn't want to make music without the knowledge of these older generations. So I set forth documenting Caffè Lena's history and cultural impact through an ambitious multimedia presentation including a book, music compilation, website, and exhibition, hoping to learn more about my craft and teaching the creative community in a bigger way.

I just didn't know that it would take me twelve years to do it.

Over the course of the project with a team of collaborators, I uncovered and reimagined archival recordings of 700 rare and live folk, blues, and jazz shows, and curated 4,000 archival photographs. This was in addition to conducting 150 oral history interviews with performers across the US. It became a vast undertaking, and I began suffering from long stretches of creative exhaustion. I was so stressed that the documentary wasn't coming together as quickly as I wanted. Patience was a really hard lesson for me. As a creative, you sometimes have this vision for how things will be and you want so badly for the pieces to come together in the way that you see it.

> It can be hard to let the project take its own form and unfold in a surprising way. But that is actually the creative process. It's not about you deciding how something is going to be—it's allowing your intention to manifest it.

When the Caffè Lena History Project did finally launch in 2013, it went on to become an internationally acclaimed award-winning project. The Caffè Lena archives are now at the Library of Congress and the project was featured in *The New York Times* and on NPR. The project's success put me on track for a production career that resulted in a Grammy Award nomination for Best Historical Album years later.

But finishing the Caffè Lena project also meant concluding years of documenting and creating. I had to come to terms with not having that anymore. You don't realize how much of your emotions and identity are in your creative work until you have to put it down.

> As much as I love change and the flow of the creative process, it was still daunting to see one chapter close while not knowing how the next would open.

I looked at the artists I was documenting and began feeling an urge to take part in the music-making process again. Until this point, I had so much of my identity caught up in being a producer that I didn't even see myself as an artist anymore.

The hardest part was just admitting to myself, "Actually, I want this." I wanted to perform again.

It was a period of reinvention and I didn't know where to start. I reflected back on when I was a young artist. I would play gigs all the time. How did I do that? I was so courageous back then. Now I found myself overthinking: "Am I still talented enough? Will people take me seriously? Are they going to think of me as only a producer?"

It was hard to put myself out there. I had to overcome colossal fears just to play one show or go to an open mic. But when I did, it felt right. In 2017, I released my latest record at the Brooklyn Academy of Music. It's amazing how when things feel right, they can still seem scary. But when you go through it enough times, you learn to trust that it's all part of the process. Creatives . . . we always jump without a net. You learn that the unexpected can be better than you thought.

It can take time for the head to catch up with the heart, but once they align, no one else's journey even matters.

Once I set out to make my own music again, I felt as though I was coming full circle and finally fulfilling the goals for myself that I had put on hold for far too long. Coming from a place of honoring artists of older generations and witnessing the dreams many left unrealized, I understood just how precious time is.

Most of us will never encounter a perfect time when we are truly ready for anything. All we have is now. So in this moment, give yourself permission to dream, to fear, to create without the burden of expectation.

Trust the process.

STAY IN THE JET STREAM.

Just be in that place where things feel good and with people who make you feel good. It sounds so simple, but being in a zone of positivity can unfold your dreams in effortless ways.

Jocelyn Arem

THE AIR OF IDEAS IS THE ONLY AIR WORTH BREATHING.

Edith Wharton

manifest

FOUNDERM

W: Win
H: Hustle
O: Ownership

EACH AND EVERY
CALL I MAKE,
I START WITH AN
INCREDIBLE LEVEL
POSITIVE EXPECTAT
AND PROSPERIT
I KNOW THAT RIGH
SOMEWHERE SOME
LIFE IS BETTE
AND MORE PROSP
BECAUSE OF
PRODUCTS AND S

MEGHAN
ASHA

Meghan Asha is CEO of FounderMade, an events platform that hosts Consumer Discovery Shows to connect consumer product entrepreneurs to retailers, distributors, and investors. She serves as an advisor and investor to startups and is a partner of the FounderMade Fund. Meghan is an on-air commentator on the latest consumer trends and technologies for CNN, the *Today Show*, and Fox Business.

FOUNDERMADE OFFICE, SOHO

186

GROWING UP,
I LIVED TO PLEASE MY
INDIAN FATHER.

I wanted to make sure his legacy of hard work carried on. More than anything, I wanted to make Dad proud. He arrived from India forty years ago with little more than a backpack and lived out the classic immigrant struggle. Dad bought a patent from HP for $2,000 when I was two and turned it into an American Dream. We went from living in an apartment to living in a house, and then living in a bigger house next to Barry Bonds after the tech company Dad founded went public. Watching his entrepreneurial journey had a profound impact on me and my desire to build.

The bar was high before I even got started. Right out of college, I had no idea what I wanted to do, but I knew Dad would be watching. So I went for the best-looking job on paper I could report back to home—finance on Wall Street. I remember walking into my hedge fund job on the first day, thinking, "I have arrived."

In reality, I was miserable. I lost myself in the long hours. More important, I was completely and utterly uninspired.

But I just kept going. I told myself that if I had an "A+ career," then Dad would love me even more. Or that if I made enough money, everything else in life would fall into place. I was living for some moment in the future when life would finally be good. But of course, the definition of "good" kept evolving each passing year.

In 2007, I got invited to a TechCrunch conference. It was the first time I had encountered so many people who created companies for a living. It blew my mind.

At the time, entrepreneurship wasn't a common path in New York City. But that one event helped me realize that this was where I belonged. These were my people. They were the pioneers of a new kind of future. I wanted to work with them, among them, and around them.

I just didn't know how to make that happen and if I did, what role I would play.

> It wasn't until years later, when I started working in venture capital, that I realized I was actually sitting on the wrong side of the table. I should be the one to build.

Build what, though?

You wouldn't believe the kinds of businesses I tried. I hated the "not knowing"—not knowing the right idea or when it would come. In the thick of it, I wrote myself a check: "$1 million for your own business." It was more symbolic than anything. In hindsight, it marked the first step of my creation journey.

I was reminding myself to believe in *me*.

I had always loved being surrounded by innovators and friends who inspired me. So I came up with an idea for a dinner series that would bring them together. It was basically "founder therapy."

The first one was at my apartment with thirty of my friends in tech and a casual speaker who shared some entrepreneurial stories. It was really bare-bones. I had no idea where this was going, but I loved it. I loved every part of it. From organizing the details of the dinner to bringing people together to connect and collaborate, it was just so fun.

My friends said, "Just follow the breadcrumbs, Meghan—you love this." I am thankful they not only saw my passion when I couldn't but also encouraged me to pursue it. Over time, the scale of these dinners grew, but my big break really came when the founder of KIND Bars, Daniel Lubetzky, agreed to be our guest speaker.

He was promoting a book release around the same time, and his PR team said that he wouldn't come for thirty people. They wanted three hundred.

Without flinching, I declared, "Done! We'll have three hundred people there!"

I hustled hard. Four hundred people showed up at the Gansevoort Hotel along with luminary keynote speakers. It became a whole new type of event experience. FounderMade was finally taking form.

I was still juggling two jobs at the time and hosted five or six more of these events before the realization hit: "OMG, this is a business! Doing what you love can actually be a business?!"

My dad attends every Consumer Discovery Show put on by FounderMade today. I never thought that simply doing what I love would bring me full circle to the entrepreneurial legacy that I grew up wanting to uphold for him.

Sticking with this venture has taught me that the path to purpose isn't always sexy. It can feel like you're navigating mundane and aimless tracks. FounderMade's humble beginning was the result of countless uneventful corporate days and consulting gigs that ultimately taught me how to execute and lead.

> FounderMade is a dream come true beyond my wildest imagination. It is surreal that all of this started as just a side hustle—a passion project that, step by step, I earned the right to pursue full-time.

Sometimes you don't even believe in yourself, but you still have to go through the motions. They could be the stepping stones to your ultimate truth. No job is too small.

Once you commit to your dreams, everything will align.

THE BEST PART OF DOING WHAT YOU LOVE AS YOUR CAREER?

You're never bored.
You achieve more fulfillment than from money
alone. Don't get me wrong—the money will
come, but the fulfillment: that is *priceless*.

Meghan Asha

BELIEVE IN YOURSELF, LEARN, AND NEVER STOP WANTING TO BUILD A BETTER WORLD.

Mary McLeod Bethune

evolve

ROSARIO
CASAS

Rosario Casas is an entrepreneur from Colombia. She is the founder and CEO of XR Americas, a workforce training platform that uses artificial intelligence, machine learning, and deep tech. Rosario has been recognized as one of the 100 Top World Disruptors in New York City by the World Summit on Innovation and Entrepreneurship. She is an advocate for women in technology and has shared her perspective on platforms such as *Forbes*, *The Huffington Post*, TEDx, Nat Geo, and more.

LONG ISLAND CITY

I REINVENTED MYSELF
IN NEW YORK CITY.

———

I'm in my forties. And I'm proof that it is never too late. In 2018, I moved from Colombia for my husband, Felipe. He received an offer to work for the Colombian Consulate in New York. At the time, I was the global CEO of Senseta, a deep tech and artificial intelligence company. Some might see leaving my career and country as a sacrifice I made for Felipe, but it was not.

My husband means a lot to me and so does my career. I believe you can value both.

Felipe is one in a million, and he knows that. Ever since we married, we prioritized taking care of each other. I know he respects me and my goals. That's why I never once questioned my decision to move for him. In fact, I saw it as an exciting challenge. We both did. It was an opportunity to reinvent ourselves, side by side.

The funny thing is, I didn't really understand what being a minority meant until I arrived in New York City. In Colombia, I spoke and acted like everybody else. But here, I found myself using English day-to-day for the first time as an adult. Thinking in English is very different from thinking in Spanish. On top of that, I was trying to establish my career in the American tech scene, which has been dominated by men in Silicon Valley.

New York was quite a culture shock. *Everything* was different, and I had to completely reimagine my life.

In Colombia, I ran a technology and innovation firm for several years. I knew exactly who to call and where to go to get business done. Here, I didn't know anyone. In fact, I couldn't work at all for six months while waiting for my US work permit to get approved. It was the worst time for me. I'm a routined person. I like structure. I want to pour myself into a job every day. But I ended up spending those first six months trying to figure out where I should even begin.

My initial plan was to pass the exams and get the permits that would put me back on the career track I had in Colombia. But I learned it would take two years. I told Felipe, "I really think that in two years, I can build my own company instead." There would be risks, of course. We wouldn't have an extra source of income. We could lose our savings. He just looked me in the eyes and said, "You have an idea. I can see it. Let's do it."

The idea was XR Americas.

During those six months of exploring my options, I became really interested in frontier technologies like big data, artificial intelligence, and extended reality (XR). At the time, there weren't many practical applications. Not many people knew how to use them. But I saw the potential these technologies could have in training large workforces and creating jobs.

In my years as a business leader, I realized that talent was far more valuable than any other resource. Creativity is infinite and it scales.

Nurturing talent can change a whole country. By 2026, new technologies and automation could force over 350 million people to reskill. I wanted to be a part of this revolution. By using spatial computing to simulate job sites, XR Americas can train a whole workforce virtually.

In South America, we used XR in capturing the aftermath of an earthquake to assist relief efforts. We also simulated equipment breakdowns to train workers in repairs. The applications are endless and the possibilities are really exciting.

What's even more exciting for me is setting an example of what Latina talent can achieve on the global stage.

I want to build a well-known brand for Colombian talent and open the door for Latinas after me.

I think this goal comes from being raised by strong women. My grandmother created the first yoga academy in Colombia back in the 1960s. She taught until she was eighty-six years old. My mother is an art critic and executive coach. All the ladies in my family are doing something entrepreneurial. They inspire me to show what Latina talent can contribute to the world.

This is my chance. It's not easy. The journey has been filled with challenges, but they don't scare me. Problems are just to-dos on your checklist. They don't define your life.

You don't know how adaptable you really are until you have no plan B. Before arriving in New York, I always thought that I wasn't a flexible person. Maybe, I was too routined.

But after following my husband here on a whim, I have completely reinvented myself. I'm still surprised at my own willpower and what I've been able to achieve despite being an immigrant, a Latina, and a woman. If something isn't working, restart. Reorganize. Try again.

> When you are clear on what you want, life works in your favor. Magic happens. A network forms around you.

My husband is the hub of my network. We are on this journey together and we have fun. We never questioned our adventure.

Over the years, I have come to realize that life shouldn't be divided between your family, mission, and career. Life is a collection of moments that are important to you. It's up to you to live each one in a brilliant way.

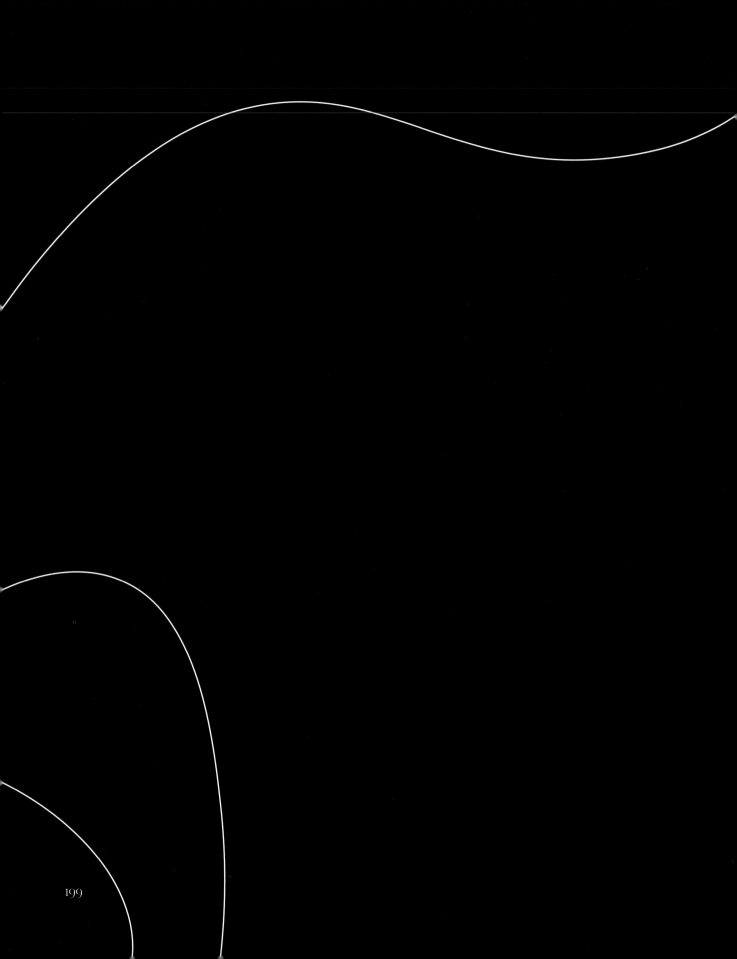

IT HELPS TO KNOW WHERE YOU ARE GOING.

I don't mean 'where' in terms of a place, a road, or a title, but where you are going in terms of a mission. When you know how you want to impact this world, you find the discipline to make things happen.

Rosario Casas

THE MOST DIFFICULT THING IS THE DECISION TO ACT, THE REST IS MERELY TENACITY.

Amelia Earhart

assured

SUSAN
DONAHUE

Susan Donahue is cofounder and Managing Partner of Skyya Communications, an award-winning strategic communications and marketing agency located in NYC and Minneapolis. She drives business for the agency and leads the business and financial press bureau as well as crisis communications for Skyya's consumer technology, automotive/ transportation, and startup companies including Polaris (NYSE: PII), Vista Outdoor (NYSE: VSTO), and mobility brands including Arcimoto (NASDAQ: FUV) and more. She lives with her husband, Conor, and their eight-year-old son, Liam Giovanni, in New York City.

EAST VILLAGE

AS A LITTLE GIRL, I WANTED TO BECOME A PROFESSIONAL BALLET DANCER.

I trained nonstop every day. Even though I had the passion and discipline to do it, my body didn't. I developed a bad left knee and a worse left ankle. When you're dancing for that many years, your body can get really battered down. It was becoming clear that my legs wouldn't take me professional—and that was really hard. I found myself at an inflection point at eighteen years old: What am I going to be about in a non-ballet world?

At the time, education seemed like a good pivot.

I hadn't set out to attend college but surprisingly, I loved it—I loved how it taught me different ways to solve a problem. Practicing ballet had honed my drive, vigor, and discipline to excel at Northeastern. So much so that in my junior year, I took the highest-paying job offer from the school's co-op program, which was an opportunity to work for a big tech company for six months and get some real work experience. I did so well there that I stayed on after the co-op ended. By senior year, I was going to school full time and working full time.

Working was incredible. I traveled all over the place, worked in other countries, and even climbed the corporate ladder. My intention was to finish my degree by taking evening courses. But then business travel picked up and I had to make a choice: Will I really need to know geology in this next stage of life?

Before the last semester of my senior year, I dropped out.

To this day, my mom asks me when I'm going to finish my degree. Being a female college dropout wasn't cool when I was coming up in my career.

For years, I felt I needed to overcompensate for the lack of a degree even though I always hit my goals and I always worked really hard—probably harder than people expected me to.

Within a few years, I became VP of Corporate Communications. But just as I moved from Boston to Minnesota to help take the company public, the dot-com bubble burst. The company went under; it could no longer make payroll. I lost my paper millions. My best friend even had to help me pay rent—twice.

I found myself at a familiar crossroad: it was time to pivot. I had amassed a big book of clients from previous engagements—it was more work than I could handle on my own.

I knew I had the discipline to win business, but at thirty-seven, I worried that I was maybe too young to start a PR agency that would be so material to the success of other companies. I had also been burned by trying to form a company with someone who ended up being a terrible business partner. But a colleague of mine at the time, Derek, really shared my vision for running a PR agency. So I mustered up the courage to walk through my fears and together, we founded Skyya.

> Despite my pivots, one thing was constant: I was a "yes" person. "Yes. Yes, I can. Yes, I'll do that." I began overcompensating and it burned me out physically and emotionally.

What people don't see is my defense mechanism—my Teflon suit. You have to have a thick skin in this business and not take things personally. Those days, I grinded hard to build my personal brand in New York City—a brand based on trust, confidence, and overdelivery.

But it was also becoming clear that by saying yes to everyone and everything, I was often saying no to me.

I worked tirelessly and did things that didn't align with my values just to keep clients happy.

Going into my forties and after years, I began to feel like I'd arrived. I had proven myself resilient through the pivots to show up as a competent and well-respected business woman, wife, and now, mother. I'd earned my right, my place, and my opinions.

> Once I learned the power of "no," there was no turning back.

The PR profession at large is probably one of the most stressful jobs out there, and you *can* burn out. I now recognize that I don't have the winning fight in me by the end of the week, so I don't typically take important business calls on Fridays. For years, my business partner would say, "Hey, Susan, you're going to have to do something on Friday." A younger Susan would reply, "Yes. Okay, sure."

Now, it's a "yes, but …" or a respectful and assertive "no."

No is power and powerful.

It doesn't mean I can't or I'm not interested. And it definitely doesn't mean I'm not capable. It's more about where I am in life. How do I want to spend my years? What do I stand for? I am a wife and a mother who works the early hours, late hours, and everything in between. I want to feel good about the businesses I'm putting out into the market. They need to feel aligned with my values.

Say what you'll do and do what you say. Understand what you need to thrive and stand by that. Be your own advocate. Give yourself permission to say no. No to overcompensating. No when it doesn't feel right. No to feeling less than.

Put the time in, learn, ask questions. But also give yourself the space to grow into your full potential, and trust that you will, even if it takes a pivot or two to get there.

HAVING YOUR OWN POINT OF VIEW AND SAYING IT OUT LOUD IS CONTAGIOUS.

I can tell exactly when I've won a client over. Ironically, it's often when I disagree with them. Saying no or having a contrarian point of view demonstrates your value more than you think.

Susan Donahue

ONE OF THE MOST CALMING AND POWERFUL ACTIONS YOU CAN DO TO INTERVENE IN A STORMY WORLD IS TO STAND UP AND SHOW YOUR SOUL.

Clarissa Pinkola Estés

purpose

hero

/ˈhirō/

A person with the courage to change the world.

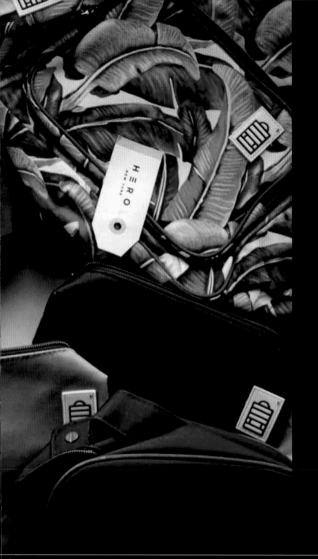

ALISSA SANDRA *BAIER-LENTZ*

Alissa Sandra Baier-Lentz is the cofounder and COO of Kintra Fibers, a materials science company that manufactures compostable biosynthetic yarns for the apparel industry. Kintra's mission is to eliminate fossil fuel-based materials and microplastic pollution from the synthetic textile value chain. Before Kintra Fibers, Alissa was the founder of HERO Backpacks, a social enterprise that created customized backpacks with empowering messages. HERO partnered with She's the First, a global nonprofit that provides education and resources to girls in low-income countries. Alissa was honored on the 2018 *Forbes* 30 Under 30 list and has since been featured in numerous publications.

TRIBECA

A HERO'S PATH IS RARELY STRAIGHTFORWARD.

———

I learned this firsthand from my grandmother. Born in rural Russia, my grandmother, Tamara, was the first woman in her family to learn to read. Tamara went on to become a doctor, despite facing years of forced labor on government-owned farms, widespread famine, political oppression, and losing her father and brothers to war.

My grandmother said her education got her through it all. She always had hope that she could build a better future with what she learned in school. My grandmother had no choice but to become her own hero.

That really stuck with me. Tamara is just one example of how educating girls creates a multigenerational impact. Education is the platform from which a girl can speak up for her rights. And yet millions of girls around the world still lack access today.

In 2016, inspired by my grandmother, I launched HERO Backpacks. Inside each HERO backpack was an empowering message, and each sale supported girls' education programs. Looking back, I thought HERO would be my legacy in making the world a better place. In reality, it was just one station on a much longer passage.

HERO eventually hit an inflection point. Order quantities increased to a level where I felt I had a responsibility to learn about the environmental impact of the materials I was using. And once that door opened for me, there was no going back.

The solutions being called sustainable often didn't make much sense. For example, rPET, which is plastic that is downcycled to yarn, has been advertised as diverting twenty billion plastic bottles from reaching the ocean. But each time you do laundry, millions of tiny plastic fibers shed from your clothes. Microfibers from these synthetics get through wastewater facilities and pollute the oceans.

Every year, our collective dirty laundry dumps microfibers into the oceans equivalent to 50 billion plastic bottles. If this rPET system pollutes more than it recycles, then why are we even doing this?

On top of all of this, eighty percent of garment workers are women—many of whom lack access to education and resources, and who are often exposed to toxic materials in production processes. This was at odds with everything that inspired me to start HERO.

I was getting frustrated. It seemed like the more I looked for answers, the more questions I had. There just had to be materials that were safer for people and the planet. Why was it so difficult to find one? I shared some of these frustrations with a mentor in the fashion industry. She suggested that maybe there was something I could contribute on a larger scale to help solve these problems. Maybe I was outgrowing HERO's original mission.

I joined an incubator and as if it were fate, I met my cofounder, Billy, almost immediately. Billy is a surfer and nano-engineer who shared my passion for designing planet-friendly products. When Billy learned about microfiber pollution, he applied his science background to solve this problem through materials development.

His research resulted in Kintra, a material that performs like traditional technical yarns, but degrades like any natural fiber. The inputs used to make Kintra are derived from sugar, not petroleum. Kintra naturally degrades in wastewater treatment plants and instead of piling up in a landfill, textiles made with Kintra can safely return to soil through industrial composting.

My intention, at first, was to help Billy connect with brands and supply chain partners, while continuing HERO. But I grew so passionate about Kintra that I quickly dove in full-time. Kintra was so energizing that I simply let curiosity drive me.

Around this time, I serendipitously heard from a non-profit that was in need of backpacks for a group of students in a rural community—one that reminded me of my grandmother's upbringing. As if it were a sign, they were seeking the exact number of HERO backpacks I had left in inventory.

In many ways, my decision to close HERO brought me even closer to the mission that launched it.

I had built HERO to empower and educate future generations. But there won't be future generations to empower and educate if we don't protect the planet, and the very communities that I was passionate about supporting through HERO are the ones most susceptible to the impacts of climate change.

Moving from HERO to Kintra felt like a natural evolution. It taught me that it's okay to change your plan. Just keep moving toward what feels right. Let your values and your learnings lead you.

No matter what challenges you face, know that every experience, lesson, trial, and triumph has its purpose. They guide you to become the hero of your own life story.

WHEN THE OPPORTUNITY TO CONTRIBUTE TO A GREATER CAUSE CALLS UPON YOU, EVEN IF UNEXPECTED, JUMP IN WITH YOUR WHOLE SOUL.

Sometimes we seek purpose, and sometimes it seeks us.

Alissa Sandra Baier-Lentz

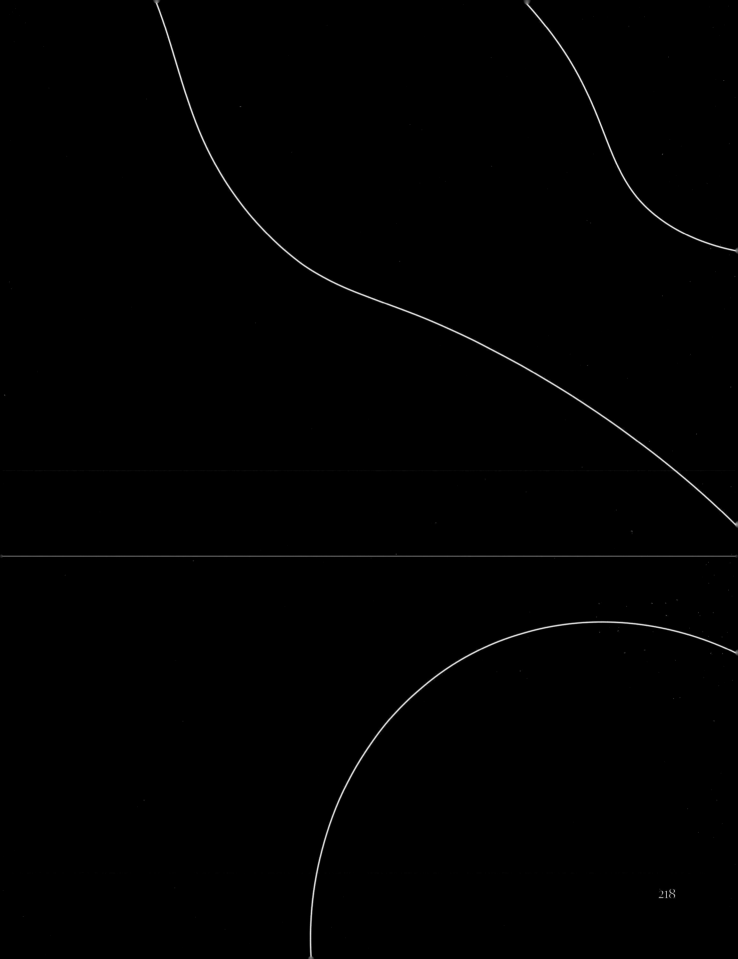

ACKNOWLEDGEMENTS

This project was made possible by a team of visionaries, artists, and friends. An enormous thanks to these talented souls. We couldn't have done it without you.

Stephanie Marshall
Designer and Creative

Anna Dobbin
Chief Editor

Amy Swanson
Proofreader and Editor

Danny Rosas
Photographer for Mahogany L. Browne and behind the scenes moments

Christopher Villano
Photographer for Palak Patel

Sharon Yang
Photographer for Batouly Camara and the authors, Ashika Kalra & Jade Chen

Dana (Coco) Vonnegut
Illustrator, New York City skyline